SELLING SUCKS
"COMMUNICATE"
TO TRIPLE YOUR PROFITS
• •
The Personal Training
Fitness Industry Edition

by Duane McGill

Contact Information
Duane McGill
Web: http://www.McGillBuilt.com
Email: Duane@McGillBuilt.com
Toll Free: (877)533-8156

Selling Sucks
Duane McGill
McNaughton-Gunn
Copyright information
Cataloging information
ISBN-10 0615377874
ISBN-13 978-0-615-37787-2

Testimonial...

Duane McGill knocked my training socks right off! When he said, "The only condition I had with the owners of this gym was, that I could fire any scum bag salesmen" Duane had been employed to come to the gym were I am a personal trainer, to help the sales team, develop their sales skills. At first I was shocked but by about 10 minutes into his presentation, he had my full attention. It was a special Saturday afternoon session he was conducting for the trainers. I could see he had a very compassionate side. His honest approach to the fitness business was refreshing. His basic philosophy was that the time had come when we the fitness world had to change our ideas on how we approached potential clients. Gone were the days were the fitness industry, would scam people out of their hard earned cash. No! His approach was honest and sensible. "Don't think of the cash you can make, but rather think on how you can help people to have a better life through proper fitness." He said.

In the past health clubs were known to sign people to long-term contracts in the hopes that the clients would never train, but pay their monthly installments for years.

Clubs would open in one town and after they took the clients money closed down and opened up with a new name in another town. But Duane's teaching was simple and honest. He taught that we, as fitness professionals, had a to adhere to a special code of conduct. Our jobs were to make people feel important. We needed to help them find the best contract that would suit them. But most of all, we needed to help people achieve their fitness goals. The fitness industry needed to change their "stinking thinking". We now had to put the potential clients needs above the basic need of making money. After the lecture I approached Duane to find He is a man who has deep religious beliefs. This was evident from the first few minutes of his lecture. I learned a lot from Duane.

I have been involved in the fitness industry for over 40 years. As a competitive Bodybuilder, Manager of the World famous (Original) Gold's Gym, contest promoter, co-founder of the A.B.A. (Amateur Bodybuilding Association), fitness lecturer (My R.E.S.T system of training), personal trainer, and writer.

But also as an Evangelist who has spoken on 4 continents. I was totally blessed that finally someone had the heart and courage to change the face of fitness, by teaching compassion, honesty and professionalism. It's safe to say in years to come many will be using Duane McGill's honest approach to fitness and calling it their own.

I fully endorse Duane McGill as an innovator in this fresh and honest approach to fitness.

- Pete Samra N.D. 1980 Natural Mr. USA.

Table of Contents

Introduction • 10
Chapter One • 14
Why are you here?
Chapter Two • 23
Crusade to Persuade (Evaluation style)
Chapter Three • 30
Build a Culture of Serving People
Chapter Four • 37
-Get Rid of Hindering-
Chapter Five • 42
The Training Team
Chapter Six • 46
Setting Appointments, Duplicate Yourself
Chapter Seven • 52
Expect your results
Chapter Eight • 58
Open Three Doors to Close One
Chapter Nine • 65
Psychology of Persuasion
Chapter Ten • 85
Ambiance of your Room
Chapter Eleven • 90
Thoughts, Feelings, Actions
Chapter Twelve • 98
The McGillBuilt 12 Step Method
Chapter Thirteen • • • • • • • • • • • • • • • • • • • 113
G.M. REPORT CARD

Introduction

The fitness industry is an incredible world. Everyone, at one time or another, has to face the reality of their mortal existence. Everyone is faced with the "get in shape or your going to be in big trouble" speech from their medical professional.

This may happen when we are young or if we are lucky, we will not hear this until we are much farther into our journey in life. Either way, we will eventually hear those spine tingling words.

The segments of people that need to hear those words, to actually do something, are just one segment of the population, about 70% to be precise.

The other 30% of the population are the segment of people that "want" to get in shape for their own reasons, not because they were told to by someone who is taking their physical health more serious than they are themselves.

Either way, the fitness industry is noticing a real boom in the market. The awareness of the great benefits that being "fit" brings to ones life is very much on the rise.

There are two reasons for this, first of all: Our "heroes" or "role models" for lack of a better description are becoming "buff", "healthy," and "fit." These are the entertainers of the world; you know who I mean; musicians, actors, and the athletes that are not supposed to be looking so "buff."

Remember when basketball players looked like basketball players and not like bodybuilders that mistakenly ended up in a gymnasium with a ball in their hand? Remember baseball players that used to be lanky guys who wore baggy uniforms? Now they have 20 inch arms that bulge out of their cloths like a man that is wearing a grade school boy's shirt.

What about the women athletes? If the athletes of 60 years ago were to come back from the dead, turn the television on and see the Williams sisters playing tennis, they would think that those "guys" have a real bad case of gynecomastia, or in bodybuilding slang "bitch tits."

Please pardon the terminology, and don't kill the messenger. I did not create that term. It has been around for as long as guys have been using those funny muscle enhancing drugs.

The Williams sisters are more muscular than any male athlete that played sports 60 years ago. Have you seen the women on the billiard tour? Yes, the billiard tour. I turned on the television the other day, and I thought the Sports Illustrated swim suit models were having a billiard play off to see who was going to make the cover of the magazine this year.

This is one of the reasons for the interest in fitness-we MUST be like our hero's and role models.

The second reason for the fitness boom is the baby boomer generation. That's right, baby boomers.

The baby boomers are the largest segment of the population and were born from 1946 to 1964. At no other time in American history have there been more people born than there was during that stretch of time- and what the baby boomers want- the baby boomers get. Since there are 8,000 baby boomers turning 60 years old everyday, guess what we want, and NEED? We want the fountain of youth, and we NEED to get "FIT," or our days being the mass of the population are numbered, and we have no intention on leaving anytime to soon.

So, no matter what side of the 70% or 30% side you are on, the fact is this-the desire to get "fit" has never been higher in American History.

There is one small problem though, other than gym class in high school, or the occasional uncle that "thinks' he knows what he is talking about, we as a society have absolutely no idea of how to really get "fit" the proper way.

We have spent the last 35 years of our lives figuring out how to make our life easier through technology. Whatever we can do, to NOT move a muscle, is considered "advanced technology."

"Look how smart I am, I discovered a way to watch a hundred different television stations without ever moving from my chair; I discovered how to stay on the couch when the phone rings – "ah," thank God for cell phones!"

"Oh yes, If I do want to shed a few pounds, I will just flip through the television stations and find an infomercial, and order a pill that will have me lose 50 lbs. by the weekend, and oh yeah, they will deliver it to my door to save me the "hassle" of getting off the couch for too long."

Well, the American population has "dummied up" to this stuff, and now realizes that there is more to "getting fit" than the crap they have been fed all these years. If they really want to get into shape, they need some help, you know: guidance, structure, and accountability.

This is were you come in, but wait not so fast; along with all that we have learned through the technology era, we have also learned how to spot a "SALES PERSON" from a mile away. We know when we walk into "ANY BUSINESS," someone is going to "attempt" to sell us something. We are on guard for this. "We are watching your every move "Mr. or Ms. Sale's person," and guess what you are doing? You are working your sales skills so you can have a better "chance," and that's all it is, a "chance" of "selling" me something."

This is why; if ten people walk through your "fitness" doors, you will be lucky to close three or four of them. In many cases that I have witnessed across the country, many "sales" people are lucky to close one or two out of ten.   Why are the numbers so pathetic? They are embarrassingly pathetic because most people try to "sell fitness."

I am going to show you how to COMMUNICATE WITH PEOPLE, and "close" at least eight out of every ten people.

Consider this; if you were sitting in front of five people and all of them spoke a different language, and only one of them spoke your language, would you be surprised if you could only "communicate" with that one person? Of course not, you would think it be foolish to communicate properly with the other four people if you couldn't "speak their language." But yet, we sit in front of people everyday of our lives and try to talk to them, sell them, deal with them, and yes, communicate with them. The silly thing is, we think just because they speak our physical language, they should understand what we are saying. This is simply crazy of us to consider. There are many personality types, many different ways in which we were raised, therefore, we are all mentally wired differently and respond differently, and frankly, we accept information in different ways.

Certain personality types are frankly horrified, irritated, and downright confused by other personality types that don't line up with theirs. So, why are we surprised that we can generally "only" sell people that are our personality types, and we cannot communicate with the others; thus leaving us with a terrible closing percentage?

Once I raise your awareness to this vital fact, you will be off and running in the new world of COMMUNICATION.

My system is guaranteed to work. I have proven my techniques all across this country. I have many, many testimonials of "professional communicators" that have double, tripled, and even quadrupled their income with my techniques of "COMMUNICATION."

Your sales days are over. "COMMUNICATE" your way to huge profits in the Fitness industry.

LET'S GET STARTED!!!

Chapter One
Why are you here?

Why are you here? I mean the real reason you are employed in the fitness industry?

Is it for the money?

Is it because you like to workout?

Is it because you like to be around people who are motivated to physically "better" themselves?

Is it because you really want to help people with their fitness goals?

All these reasons can be very accurate, but done in the wrong order; these reasons can really back fire on you.

If you are in the fitness industry only for the money, you will probably do some very unscrupulous things to make your money. This is why, if you are here for the money, and you could care less if you work here for a dollar, or down the road at the local Wal-Mart for a dollar; the people that are dependant on your "fitness expertise" will generally feel this "lack" of sincere caring for their health. This, in turn, will make it difficult to close deals. As I stated before, people can smell a sales person a mile away.

Therefore, you will have to, let's say, stretch the truth a little, or a lot, in order to get a sale. I have been around the fitness industry for over 30 years, and I have SEEN IT ALL.

I have witnessed many, many good people, who have entrusted their local "fitness expert" with their goals and dreams, only to get, what I consider to be a cruel joke played on them. The person that sold them a gym membership, or more importantly, PERSONAL TRAINING, had just set them up for failure.

The sales person had no intention of helping the client fulfill their goals and dreams of being physically fit.

The sad thing is this; everyone that "wants" or "need" to fulfill their fitness aspirations, is really doing it for emotional reasons far more than physical reasons. "Your body won't go where your mind hasn't been first."

The toll on the client's mind from the lack of results that they believed was going to happen, well, let's just say, I have seen some very disturbing actions from these people; depression, anger, and a sense of hopelessness that can stay with them forever.

This is not a game here. We should all be in the fitness industry because we REALLY want to help people reach their goals.

Before you are through with this book you are going to learn how absolutely critical it is to attach an "emotional feeling" to the "physical result" your client wants to get from their fitness experience.

I will promise you this; "people get a feeling, then they purchase the feeling." "Facts and figures make you think; emotion makes to act."

When you realize the depth of the emotional impact that your promises have on your client, you will do two things:

Number one-you will have a clear understanding why I am going to make you a "Master Communicator" of a person's emotional "needs" and "wants."

Number two-you will handle this privilege with kid gloves.

When you realize the magic in understanding the "psychology of human emotions" you will be able to persuade your clients to follow your every word.

This is where the privilege and responsibility comes in. You must respect the fact that you are a "professional communicator," and people will listen to you, and follow your every word because they trust you. You should never abuse this gift. A person's emotions are very, very serious. Playing with them is nothing short of criminal.

I am coming at you a little hard right now for two reasons:
One reason - if you are getting offended by my insinuations of your ethics, then you are probably a person that needs to look in the mirror, and ask a few questions to yourself in this area.

Reason two - I hope all the people, that are not the upstanding, ethical, caring, and "people loving" individuals that I am trying to reach; well, frankly, I hope they all put this book down, so I can only work with the upstanding, ethical, caring, and "people loving" individuals that I wrote this book for.

I really do not want anyone reading this material that will abuse this knowledge. I have the absolute best communicative techniques in the fitness industry, they should only be applied by people that will respect, and use them, with the up most responsibility.

-No sales people wanted-

The first thing I do when I go into a fitness facility is get rid of the sales people.

You heard me right, companies pay me big dollars to come in, evaluate, re-organize staff, and train their employees. The first thing I do is get rid of the sales people.

I have taken fitness centers from grossing $1000, to having them gross (in personal training) sales $40,000 in a two week time frame. This means from the time I walked into the building, the gross revenue went from $1,000 to $40,000 in the following two weeks.

I did this by firing the sales people. I kept, or hired the people that really cared about the client base. You know who I am talking about, the people that are ethical, caring, and people loving.

These people are very easy to recognize, they are always making sure their clients are happy and well taken care of. They are also the people that ALWAYS say, "I could never be a sales person."

Bingo, that's my person. That's the one that I want to teach my techniques to. That's the one that will be well on their way to making a six figure income; that's a minimum of $100,000 a year.

I have done it many times, and I am going to continue to find these caring individuals for the rest of my life.

I take these people and make "communication professionals" out of them. I erase the "sales person" stigma, and teach them to do what they are really supposed to be doing, which is "COMMUNICATING" to their client, the value of their service. At this point, their client can see how that "value" can impact their lives. Thus, the "value" of the service that is being "communicated," becomes a "value" to the client.

I will ask you this, do you think a person that joins a fitness facility is better off just training on their own?, or do you really believe that the person would get far more benefits if they received guidance, structure, and accountability by someone like YOU?

If you really think that a normal person that joins a fitness center could get the same results by exercising by their self, instead of having your professional guidance, then of course, you are definitely in the wrong business.

On the other hand, if you are the kind of person that believes, without a shadow of a doubt, that not just the normal person, but everybody would absolutely benefit far more by having a professional trainer, such as yourself, be by their side to help them reach all their fitness, and emotional goals, then why in the world would you be thinking that you are selling them anything?

You are giving them the opportunity to get far better results than they could possibly get on their own. If a person were dying of thirst, and you owned a water stand, I am quit sure you would not be thinking, "Gosh, I really don't want this person to think I am pushy or too forward. I mean, if he really wanted some water, he would tell me, wouldn't he?" Sound familiar?

Let me tell you why we have this innate thought about this situation.

We are all brought up to view "sales people" as BAD. I mean, for the most part, we have definitely not been brought up to say, "Yippee, there is a sales person. I sure hope he will "talk me" out of the money I have in my pocket, so I can go home and regret what he just sold me." No, no, we steer away from those people until we need them, sort of like policeman. We want nothing to do with them, until we really have to deal with them, but even then, we still aren't very comfortable around them.

Now, fast forward to your adult life-you're out looking for a job, you find all kinds of options, but you really want to get into the fitness industry. Why? Because you really like to exercise, you like people, you like to be around people that are motivated, and you would love to help people reach their fitness goals.

"O.K., I guess I need to work the front counter, you know, just basically handing out bottles of water, protein shakes, and energy drinks. I can do this – this is easy."

I use the term handing out, because to say there is any "selling" involved in this, is like saying that you sell Big Macs at McDonald's-you are an order taker, period!!

"Maybe I can be a trainer; that would be fun! Yes, I think I am going to be a trainer."

Off to work you go- now you are a trainer. Well, as the days go by, you are introduced to the SALES PERSON. THE BIG UGLY, you think to yourself, "I could never be a sales person, I would hate to feel like I am bugging people, or being pushy; If they would like to by training, then they will ask me for it – right?"

Of course, little do you know, the clients you're currently training; are there because of the sales person.

You see, the reason even so called good sales people have a hard time having an endless amount of prospective clients sitting with them, is this-when you view yourself as a sales person, you automatically have a bad "picture" of yourself in your head. This is because you have always thought of sales people as bad, or at least pushy.

We, as an American culture, seem to think if you are aggressive, fast talking, pushy, quick witted, "are a great bull shitter," hard closer, and "never take no for an answer" kind of person, then you will make a great sale person.

This is SO NOT how the truly great sales people act. The sales profession is the most lucrative profession in the World. This being the case, why do most of the sales people we know live paycheck to paycheck, and bounce around to different industries looking for the "right one?"

They go to an industry, blow the thing apart, in terms of "selling." By this I mean, they produce good sales numbers very quickly, then, before you know it, they're gone, on to the next gig, leaving behind a trail of disaster and complaints from their last job.

Or, they get promoted, at the same place that they blew up those great sales numbers, and fall flat on their face as a manager because they really have ZERO people skills. To manage people, you need people skills; in fact to "sell" effectively, you need people skills.

These people are what we call "slick Willie" sales people; you know exactly the ones I am talking about.

These are the people, which we as an American company, think we need to hire in order to have our product or service effectively "sold" to the consumer.

Getting back to why, if the sales industry is the most lucrative industry in our country, why are so many sales people starving? This is why; those people are just sales people. They are not professional communicators, they have zero people skills, they talk more about themselves than they do the customer, and they are WORRIED about MAKING THE SALE.

This is the absolute worst person that you can have in your company. The professional "sales person" that makes the big bucks, does everything with the prospective client other than "SELLS THEM!!"

This person doesn't jump job to job, looking for the next big thing. This person makes well into the six figure range, often more in the range of $200,000 than $100,000.

This person can run a sales staff of any amount, because he or she has phenomenal "people" skills, and has a clear understanding of what is really important to the client. By the way, what is important to the prospective client IS NOT having you feed them a line of crap so they will buy from you, so you can get a commission, then run home and pay your electric bill before it gets shut off.

I did get a little off course here. Let's get back to what happens when you have a "bad picture" in your head of what the "sales person" image is.

You instantly and automatically have reservations about approaching people on the fitness floor, or calling them on the phone, because you have "labeled" yourself a salesperson. So, now you must manifest the feelings of a sales person. You start to think, "I know this lady thinks the only reason I want to talk to her is because I want to "SELL" her personal training." "I know this person thinks that I am calling him on the phone because I am trying to "SELL" him personal training."

So, you start to dread going to work, because you are viewing yourself as a "con man."

You need to change your paradigm to what you are really there to do; which is to "COMMUNICATE" the "value" of your service, so your prospective client can see how that will impact their lives, thus the "value" of the service that you are "communicating" becomes attached to your client's "value system." "We all have a set of values, and through those values, we filter our reality, if we are doing things that are in conflict with our value system, we will "self defeat," and "sabotage" the situation." This will not be the only time in this book that you will hear this. You must "line-up" the value of your service, with your client's value system, period!

QUIT SELLING AND START COMMUNICATING the value of how you can change their lives. If you don't believe in the value of what you are communicating, then find another area of life that you do believe in. Start to share and communicate that information, so you can feel proud of yourself, and quit looking at yourself as a pushy sales person. Only the lowest forms of life would feel good about that image of themselves. I wouldn't wish that "picture," of one's self, on a good hearted person that really cares for people. If you look at what you are really doing in the fitness industry, you will see that you really are changing people's lives for the better. In fact, if it wasn't for you, most of them would have quit the fitness center.

Do you realize that 42% of all the people that join a fitness center, become "inactive," and quit coming to the center within the first 30 days of joining?

Do you realize how many people you have kept in the fitness center by being there for them, providing structure, guidance, accountability?

You truly are a vital part of their success-be proud of that. Hold your head high. Quit viewing yourself as a "sales person" and start viewing you as a "communicating professional." You are someone who cares enough about the clients "wants," and "needs" that you are willing to learn to do whatever it takes to communicate the value of your service, so your client will realize how valuable it will be for them in their lives.

I believe in what you have to offer them, and you obviously do to, or you wouldn't have read this far.

Let's do this thing-let's go!!!

Chapter Two
Crusade to Persuade
(Evaluation style)

• •

Guidance, structure, and accountability- all the things we love to hate. Athletes love to hate it. Movie stars love to hate it. Musicians love to hate it, and anyone that is striving for a worthy goal loves to hate it.

When all is said and done, and the goal has been accomplished; the pats on the back, and all the praises for a job well done have been expressed- there you are- giving thanks to all the people that helped you through it.

Then you give special thanks to that one person - the glue that held it all together. That person you couldn't stand, or at times hated. They made you continue when you thought you had nothing left, and you just wanted to rest. This person was on your tail all the time, seemingly enjoying the anguish of your pains. When you didn't think you could take another step, this person gave you the courage to go on. They knew how badly you wanted to reach your goal, and they were determined to make sure that you didn't "get in your own way."

When you stood there in all your glory, there was one person in the room happier for you, more so, than you were yourself. In the fitness industry we call this person "YOUR PERSONAL TRAINER." The guidance wielding, structure oriented, accountability driven freak show, this person would rather lose an arm than see you fail.

This is why I am on a "crusade to persuade" everyone that enters a fitness facility to have a personal trainer to help them reach their goals.

Let's dispel a few rumors about personal trainers.

1. Personal trainers always scream at you and make you feel so much pain, that you want to die. FALSE. Personal trainers guide and instruct you, as well as push you to levels that you can handle. Levels that you would generally not push yourself to, but they also understand your limits.

2. Personal trainers are big ugly monsters with 20 inch arms, regardless if they are a guy or a girl. FALSE. Personal trainers are highly educated people in the area of physical fitness. They study all the latest discoveries in the fitness industry, to ensure maximum results for their clients. They are also very fit, and practice what they preach.

3. Personal trainers are only needed by people that don't know what they are doing, or are too "weak minded" to help themselves. FALSE! Professional athletes, all across the World, have personal trainers. Personally, I won two National Championships in Powerlifting, and I NEVER entered a contest unless my trainers schedule was in line with mine. I needed my trainer's guidance, structure, and accountability as much as anyone else did.

When I worked in fitness centers across the country, my job was that of general manager, also known as, a fitness director. I was the person who made sure the trainers had plenty of clients. This was a very easy process, due to my strong belief in the value of personal trainers. My goal was to make sure everyone in the club knew the value of a personal trainer. What I found, is that many people can't get out of their own way. What I mean is this; people have a great way of rationalizing (rationing lies) to themselves that they can get the results they are looking for, on their own. I knew better. You will never convince me of that. I don't care how much you know about getting fit, if you are really serious about getting great results- you need a trainer.

What eventually would happen, was the prospective client that walked out my door, not having joined my training team, (I will cover the "training team" concept in an upcoming chapter) would eventually quit coming to the club.

All of us, who have been in the fitness industry for any length of time, have seen this take place: A person joins the fitness center with all the best intentions; they have their goals firmly established in their heads, they know what they want to look like, and they are excited to get started.

Day one, the person walks into the club, starts to get comfortable with the equipment, and reads the instructions on the machines. Of course, the machines give you no instruction on proper hand placement, proper breathing techniques, or a structured routine to go by, etc, etc. The person works out- by their definition- goes home and looks in the refrigerator for that healthy "after work out" nutrition, of which they know nothing about. They do this for about two or three weeks, just long enough to still be sore, but yet, see no results.

The person does a quick review of their progress. They see that they are taking time to go to the club. They are feeling like they have gotten run over by a truck, they are making a major effort in "watching" what they eating, yet, they have absolutely no clue on what to "watch" for. They haven't seen any results in this "lengthy" time period- you know, from the beginning, to the whopping two to three week period. They get depressed, and then find 20 reasons why they just do not have the time to come to the club anymore.

Now, does this sound familiar to any of you personal trainers? I thought so. I literally felt like I was letting them down if I didn't do whatever I could to show them the value of having a personal trainer.

I knew most of them were going to end up quitting the club, because they got depressed and discouraged. I was personally responsible for their existence in the club; I had almost full control in keeping them a part of our workout family. The service I had to offer, was going to keep them healthy, and living a much better quality of life. I took this responsibility very seriously.

I have been around the fitness world for over 30 years. I know the value of feeling great about myself. I know that, me feeling great about myself, is the main reason that I have been successful throughout my life. Whenever anything or everything went "kaput" in my life, I always had the fitness center to go to. I could just go there and let it all hang out. I could look in the mirror and say, "You know Duane, no matter what is going on in your life, you still look great and have your health. Everything else will work its way out."

This is why I was on a crusade to persuade to get as many people as I could to join my personal training team, and I was going to get as creative as I could. I was determined to develop a system that would make it obvious to my prospective clients that they badly needed the services of my personal trainers. I was going to develop a system that was so emotionally driven, that they couldn't wait to have one of my trainers work with them.

I did develop such a system- people all across the country use it to help people reach their physical and emotional goals.

We will be diving deep into the 12 step method portion of this system in chapter twelve. But first we must continue our journey into what it takes to have a top notch professional personal training business. I will give you a small hint – DO NOT SELL PERSONAL TRAINING!

-FITNESS EVALUATION-

That's right! – Quit selling personal training! Personal training is a debt, not a goal. If you are asking people if they want to purchase some personal training, you are really asking them if they want to spend money, be inconvenienced, and have sore muscles. This is why most fitness clubs and personal trainers are going broke.

Listen, if I asked you if you wanted to run into a burning house, just for the heck of it; what would you tell me? ABSOLUTELY NOT! – Right? What if I ask you if you wanted to run into a burning house to get your kids out, now what would you tell me? ABSOLUTELY YES!!! – This is the same situation (burning house), but totally different answers when asked a different way. One reason was attached to an emotional feeling, and one reason wasn't. I will show you how to have more personal training clients than you ever thought possible, but you must promise me one thing – you will not sell personal training!

Do fitness evaluations! I don't' mean just any fitness evaluation. If fact the evaluations that I have witnessed in fitness clubs around the World, are rather embarrassing, and intolerable to watch.

O. K. let's review a "normal" fitness evaluation. People sign up to the fitness center, a personal trainer may or may not set down with that person. If they do, the trainer will tell them all about the cool stuff the club has to offer, including "personal training," they might check their body fat or B.M.I (body mass index), then they take them to the workout area for a quick routine, and then, they bring them back to the office and put a personal training price sheet in their face. "Here are our prices, how many sessions do you want to Buy?" – SOUND FAMILIAR?

I am talking about an official fitness evaluation. This evaluation is detailed, and tailored to the client's physical and emotional needs. NOTE: As I discuss the fitness evaluation in the later chapters, I will be using the terms "evaluation" and "presentation." For the purpose of discussion – these terms have the same meaning.

The number one biggest mistake in the fitness industry is having unequipped "human behavior" specialist's "selling personal training." This is usually the club owner, front counter staff, and most definitely the personal trainers.

The paradigm of the fitness industry needs to entirely change, when viewing this issue. There are, collectively, millions of dollars lost every day in the fitness industry because of this "backward" approach. As I have stated, 42% of people that join a fitness club, end up quieting within 30 days.

Most people who get personal training actually seek out personal training; this is about 5% of the average clubs member base. The other 95% is where the money is!

When you have a systematic way to set appointments, which will allow you to give fitness evaluations to 90% of your member base – NOW your talk' in!

Not only is this where the money is – IT'S THE RIGHT THING TO DO! These people need the help more than anyone else in your club. When a fitness club has a solid evaluation system, two things happen: all the members of your club have the opportunity for guidance, structure, and accountability. And the profit center of the personal training department will go through the roof.

I have put the McGillBuilt 12 Step Method, which is an evaluation method, in fitness clubs across the Country, and the results have ALWAYS been phenomenal – not good – PHENOMENAL!

If a fitness club is "selling" a couple of thousand dollars a month of personal training, and they call me to help their situation – I will go to the club, IMMEDIATELY take down any personal training advertising, implement my 12 step method "evaluation" process, and in a matter of weeks (meaning one or two), I will have the club generating $30,000 to $40,000 dollars of personal training each and every month. GUARANTEED!

This is why my material is distributed in 87 Countries around the World.

That was just one example. I have been in clubs that only sign up 15 to 20 new members a month, to the club itself, and they are not "selling" any personal training at all, and within a week or two of implementing my method, the club will generate $15,000 to $20,000 dollars of personal training, month after month.

Although I am not beyond bragging a little bit – I really am telling you this because I am sick and tired of watching good people be "forgotten." These people really need our help, if they ever expect to reach their physical and emotional goals. I am also sick and tired of watching hard working fitness club owners and personal trainers, lose their business's because of "missing the mark" on how to maximize their personal training member base. This has to STOP – to many great people, from both sides of the fence are suffering.

Start evaluating your members, all members! You will see a dramatic increase in member retention, as well as personal training growth.

Chapter three is going to help you change your paradigm, when it comes to viewing your club as a "help' center, as oppose to a fitness club. This concept will work hand in hand with your evaluation program that you are going to implement. It's time to get serious about helping all the people in your club – LET'S GO!

Chapter Three
Build a Culture of Serving People

Building a culture of "serving people" is the most important "first step" in building your career in the fitness industry.

When doing this, your total focus is to make sure all the people in your club are reaching their goals, regardless of whether they buy personal training from you or not. When you walk into your fitness club, you should be thinking of serving people in the form of better health.

"People do not care how much you know until they know how much you care." When you walk into your club you should be revered as a life saver of sorts; people should feel comfort when you are in the club.

When you walk into your doctor's office, and you have some medical issues that need attention, you definitely feel better when you "physically see" the doctor - Even if you are walking into the examination room, and you catch a glimpse of the doctor as he passes by. The doctor hasn't even sat down with you yet, but you still have a sense of comfort- everything is going to be O. K.- "The doctor is here."

This is the same feeling the members of your club should feel every time they see you, either up close, or at a distance. They know that if they need any help, you are there for them.

The head of the personal training department should be the most sought after person in the club. The position should have the image of: help, guidance, structure, and accountability. In most clubs, however the head of the personal training department's image is that of: SALES PERSON, pressure, "talk to you if there is money to be made," and sales quotas. This is a lousy feeling to have to live with every day. It's like how many people view the site of a police officer, "Why are they here in our area, they must want something, pretend like you don't see them."

My father was a policeman for 18 years, and I can tell you this-the image that he had, was entirely unfair. Most policemen are there to help, they are great people. The same goes for the head of the training department. If the position isn't viewed that way, then you are absolutely doing something wrong.

Doing something wrong in the personal training department can cost you a lot of money.

-HAPPY HOUR-

Happy hour means generally one thing; go to the bar after work, hang out with you friends, have a few drinks, and talk about the misery of the day!

Let's review this situation; go to a bar equals spending money. Drinking alcohol equals a ruined body. Hanging out with friends, often equals talking about all the negative things in your life, or listening to their sad story.

O. K., let's look at another form of happy hour. Coming to the fitness center equals good physical health, good mental health, and good emotional health. Hanging out with people in a fitness club, often equals talking about how to achieve a more defined body, higher energy level, and pointers on how to relieve stress. Now this is a REAL "HAPPY HOUR."

For many people, their workout time is the biggest part of their day. This is THEIR time. How much of the day can you really consider YOUR TIME? I mean really, doesn't most of your day consist of GIVING to others? - giving to a spouse, children, career, friends, and bill collectors. God bless them; but come on- we all need our PER-

SONAL TIME.

Unfortunately, many people find this in the form of drinking at happy hour or sitting home on their favorite spot on the couch, staring at the television, trying to disconnect themselves from anything and everybody in their lives.

The exercise enthusiast is a very unique person. I have stated several times, that I have been in and around fitness centers for over 30 years, and I can honestly say, that exercise enthusiast's really are unique people, they view life through a different set of glasses; a better set in my opinion.

The fitness club is their happy hour, and it means a lot to them. We are there to make sure they have the best possible time while they are with us in our world. I think we often take it for granted just how lucky we are for being able to work in an atmosphere that we love. Many people don't have that luxury; they are in jobs, and environments that they can't stand. They are often depressed, angry, tense, and frustrated over many things in life; the least we can do for them is make their time with us as enjoyable as possible.

Have you ever been to a restaurant, theme park, or any place were you were trying to relax and unwind from the day, and the customer service people treated you like you were absolutely ruining their day by being there? We have all been through this; that's a lousy feeling isn't it? We are often the "energy" for our members. They come to the club to relax, relieve some stress, and have something to look forward to. The least we can do is to welcome them with open arms. This is what makes the fitness culture different than any other. The physical, mental, and emotional benefits that people receive can be found nowhere else. Let's make sure we give people the best possible experience; as Zig Ziglar said, "When you give enough people what they want, you will always have everything that you want."

-TRAIN PEOPLE FOR FREE-

If you want to make more money, train people for free! I know what you are thinking- "O. K. now, what the heck is going on here? Train people for free?" Sure, why not!

Let me explain something to you. You are your own advertisement when you are walking the club floor. You can put up fliers, fish bowl contest's, or even have your trainer's walk around the floor with neon signs on their back, but nothing is better advertisement than walking the floor and helping people workout.

Now, I don't necessarily mean, work people out for their entire session, but I do mean help them with certain movements they are doing wrong (which is most of them). Show them some good exercises for that "hard to build" body part, you know the one. The body part that no matter what they do, it just doesn't respond like all the others do. We all have one of these body parts, ask them which body part is the toughest for them to get in shape, and you will get an answer 100% of the time.

Listen, what else are you doing if you are not communicating to someone in your office that personal training is the best thing that people can do for themselves? You should be out on the floor communicating- by your actions- that personal training is the best thing that people can do for themselves.

I earned tens of thousands of additional dollars from my club members, because I worked the floor and shared my knowledge and expertise. Did the people that I was showing the "tricks of the trade" to, sign up for training? Often yes, but I had more people sign up that were "watching" me show someone else how to train better. You see, people are always watching you. Clearly understand, people have their eyes on you all the time. We think for some reason that all people are free spirits, fun loving, and outgoing. This simply isn't true. Many people are very reserved; they are not going to just walk up to you because you have a title.

People need to see that you are a friendly person that REALLY CARES ABOUT THEM. When you are on the floor helping people, other people that need help, but simply will not normally approach you, will start to feel comfortable with you, even though they have never talked with you. They see that you are helping everyone. I cannot tell you how many times I had these people knock on my office door and say, "Hi there, I was wondering if you could answer a few questions for me."

I will say it again, "People do not care how much you know, until they know how much you care."

Please, do not misunderstand me. The people that I was directly helping with new exercises and positions also joined the training team many times. This is what I would say after showing someone a few things that helped them get closer to their goals. I would say, "Good job on doing that movement Joe (or what ever); you may want to consider joining the training team."

This is a hypnotic language pattern that is very user friendly. It's not pushy; you are simply suggesting an idea that will help them reach their goals. People are very receptive to this kind of dialog. I say this as I am walking away. I do not wait for an answer; I am simply planting seeds.

People buy things from people they like, this is an absolute fact. Be part of the fabric of your club, don't just be an "order taker" for people that "want" personal training. Develop that "want" and that "need." Your clients deserve that. They don't know what their missing, it should be your mission to help them see the value.

-WALK TO THE BATHROOM-

If you want to know if you are doing a good job in your quest to be ingrained into the fabric of your club, walk to the bathroom. If you can't make it to the bathroom without being stopped by more than a few people, you are doing a good job.

When you are respected and admired in your club for being a difference maker in people's life, people will look for reasons to talk to you. If the bathroom is far away from were your office is, just take a walk and see how many times you get stopped. People will want to talk to you for seemingly the silliest reasons-Nice weather today! Did you see that game last night? How are things going in the club today? And of course, I have had to slow down a little bit because of this nagging shoulder, back, or knee. People just want to know that you are accessible, just in case they need that pointer, or bit of information. They also like to feel that they are in the "know." That they are in the inner circle, your inner circle; if anything is going on in the club, they want to feel like you would let them know.

This is a good thing. This shows that they see you as a leader in the club, and not just a "sales person." You have become a staple mate in the club. When they are talking to their friends that are not members the fitness club, perhaps they live in another city, you can rest assured that you are well known to their friends. You wouldn't know them if they were sitting next to you, but they know all about you.

I was in a club in The Carolina's and the "sales manager" had been fired a couple of weeks before I arrived. I was talking to some of the club members, and they didn't realize that he was gone!! WOW!! Now, this guy obviously had not read my book. This guy is probably at another job telling everyone how lousy the club was, and that he just quit (It's his story, he will tell it the way he wants) because there was no "money" to be made. Yet, no one had any idea he even worked there, or certainly didn't care that he left.

You need to "be your club"- You are the identity- you are why people stay and bring in their friends and family. I promise you this, people do not bring their friends and family to be sold by someone; they bring them in to meet a great person, and someone that can help them with their goals and dreams-that someone is you!!

Chapter Four
-Get Rid of Hindering-

• •

Let me tell you about an event that happened to me while I was working with a company in Mobile, Alabama. I was there on a mission to clean the place up, from the stand point of morale, enthusiasm, and of course sales numbers.

I went into this fitness club; a beautiful club, it was about 75,000 square feet, marble floors, waterfalls, big theatre just like at the IMAX- awesome place.

Well, the owners of this personal training company were losing their butts on the sales end of the personal training program. Here they were in this beautiful club, as nice as any in the country, yet the sales were terrible, and the atmosphere was even worse.

I walked into the club, as I always did, as a person coming in for the first time. I was starting to workout, just minding my own business. I looked around to see if I could find the head of the personal training department and his any trainers. I found both. The trainers were at the juice bar just shooting the breeze, and the head of personal training department was playing on the computer.

I was there for about 40 minutes working out by myself. I was never approached by anyone, let alone anyone from the training department. I proceeded to go up to the juice bar to get a drink and to see if any of the trainers would at least make a move on the topic of personal training. Not a word was mentioned. I thought, well, I guess I will start the conversation. I said, "Hey man-how is the personal training in this place?" "Well, its ok, it could be better." WHAT!!! A trainer said, "It's ok, it could be better!" A trainer said that!!!

As you can imagine, I just about lost it. You must remember that this club is worth several millions of dollars just in the building and equipment. They had 15 trainers on staff, and one of them told me "the training is ok but it could be better." O. K., maybe this trainer is just an idiot, maybe he's a new guy who has no couth at all. As I really pressed for some attention on personal training, I finally told him who I was and why I was there. Oddly enough, he didn't seem to be too fazed. Even stranger was the fact that this personal trainer was one of the best trainers this club had; he had been there since the club opened 6 years ago!

Wow!! I thought I had seen it all!!

Well, it was time to introduce myself to the sales manager. Oh boy-was this ever a treat. This guy was the most negative person I had met in a long time. He reeked of bad attitude.

This guy had every excuse in the world why he couldn't sell training in this club. I was literally getting sick to my stomach listening to him. "The weather is too nice, people don't have money, people think they can train on there own, blah, blah, blah."

"It doesn't matter where you are on the outside; it matters where you are on the inside." This guy failed mentally, long before he had a chance to fail physically.

The clients and employees of the club couldn't stand to be around this guy, he sucked the energy right out of them. They knew he was there for one reason and one reason only-give me your frickin' money or get out of my face.

Now, you might think, "WOW, of course people are going to be turned off if you exude that kind of attitude. But wait a minute-this guy was pretty forward in this manner." Don't think for a minute that just because you put on a nice smile (fake), that people can't feel right through that. Please, do not think you are fooling anyone. Your true feelings really do show themselves.

When you understand how energy works in this universe you will soon realize that acting like you "care" will get you just as financially broke as blatantly showing your true colors.

"It isn't what you tell people you think, or what they think you think, it's what you really think, deep inside, that will determine your success or failure." You will attract to you that which you are resonating with. If you really do not think that you can get people to join your training team, then you will attract people that do not want to join. It's as simple as that.

For a more in-depth understanding of this universal law, I would strongly encourage you to read my book "Positive Thinking Sucks, Internalization Rules."

Anyway, as I continued with my review, it was obvious why this club was doing terrible in the morale, enthusiasm, and income side. This guy took the cake. After I spent about an hour with this guy, believe me, that was more than enough, I was walking out the door and another gentleman came up to me and said, "Hello, my name is Ken. I was wondering-who do I talk to about putting in my two weeks notice?" I said, "What do you do here?" Ken proceeded to tell me that he was the assistant manager of the personal training department. Ken also told me that he wasn't making any money here, and the head sales manager was really negative. I said, "YA THINK?" I asked Ken to give me a couple of days to work with him (meaning ken), and If he still wanted to quit after that, then I understood.

Ken agreed. The next day I spoke with the district manager of the personal training division. He handled this club, and three others. His name was Josh Cepek, a phenomenal young man who had just taken over the district a short time before.

Josh and I proceeded to talk about the situation with his sales manager "Mr. Motivation." Josh agreed with me, that firing the manager was the best thing to do. Josh fired the manager the next day. Josh took some heat from his boss's at corporate, due to the lack of any understanding in the "common sense" department. Some Corporate staff members were not really happy with the fact that this guy sold $20,000 of personal training in a two week period and Josh fired him.

Now, this may sound like a lot of money, but the club goal was $40,000 in a two week pay period. I told you this club is big. The Corporate staff wanted me to go to Mobile to fix things, but apparently, that didn't mean get rid of people that were really "hindering" the ability of the good people.

Well, this feeling was short lived. From the day that manager was no longer in the building, the atmosphere was a thousand times better. You could literally feel the difference. As far as the situation with Ken went; Ken and I worked together about three days, not a lot of time, but enough for Ken to see an entirely different view of how a club should be ran.

Ken was a great guy; he really cared for the clients in his club. He was service first, sales second. Ken had never sold more than $8,000 of personal training in a two week period before I came to "get his head on straight." This was the fifth day of the month when I came to meet Ken. He only had until the 15th of the month to get his sales numbers done. Now that Josh had made Ken the head sales manager, Ken's club goal was $40,000. Remember, previous manager- the negative nitwit, could only do $20,000 a pay period on his best performance. Ken had already ZEROED the first five days, working under the negative nightmare he called his boss. So, what were the chances that Ken could pull off $40,000 in the next ten days?

Well, Ken did the "impossible," he sold (communicated) $42,000 of personal training in ten days. He ended the pay period as the number one sales person in the company. Ken sold $46,000 of personal training the following two week pay period. Ken followed my system to the letter. Why not? Ken was making a whopping $800 a pay period, what did he have to lose? Oh yeah, Kens check for "communicating" to his clients the value of personal training; was ten times that of his normal pay.

Ken was just the kind of person that I wanted to work with. The great thing about that situation was that Josh was Ken's supervisor. Once Ken "saw the light," Josh was able to help him stay on track. Josh and I had worked together months before at some other clubs in Nebraska. I knew Josh's potential, that's why I went to Mobile to help out.

"Getting rid of the hindering" in your club is absolutely vital. You are losing thousands of dollars a week by having that negative stench in the club. I know it doesn't seem like it, but when you get rid of this type of person once, you will never allow that type of person to work in your club again.

Chapter Five
The Training Team
• •

Well, I have previously made mention of the "training team." This is as vital as anything you will incorporate into your club. People love to be a part of a team; a bowling team, softball team, billiards league, antique car club, poker night with the boys, or golf team.

There are clubs, associations, and teams for almost everything we want to get involved in. People love to associate with other people. They love to be a part of something. Why shouldn't it be the same with getting fit? Why do this alone? Why not have a group of people that you are associating with that have similar goals and dreams? This is exactly why people join other associations, clubs, and teams.

You could say, "Well, they did join a club when they joined the fitness center! Why would they need to join another club within a club?" They joined the club because they wanted to be around people that were striving for the same thing they were. Ask your self this; why do kids that go to college still join fraternities? Why do people that have a summer pass to the local golf course still join the golf league? Why do people that bowl all the time feel like they have to be on a bowling league? People "need" more of an inner connection with people that are really serious about the goals of their heart. Just being in the room where the event is taking place doesn't do it. Call it what you will, but people love being involved in a team.

Psychologically speaking, there is comfort in numbers for people; if enough people are doing it, it must be O. K. People will do the strangest things when it comes to the group. People will work harder for a group. People will be on time far more so for a group, and to a large degree, people are more apt to want to succeed more for the group than they would for themselves.

The neat thing about the team concept is that obviously your clients are not going to be necessarily working out with other people that they do not know. You are their team, along with the other people that are training at the same time of the day as they are, but with different trainers. The client has the comfort of privacy with you, and also, if they choose to, they can mingle with the people that are training on the team at the same time. It really does make for a "come on we are all in this thing together" concept. People do not feel like they are the only ones that need a trainer. Again, there is comfort in numbers. How many times have you been asked by a prospective client, "Are there a lot of people that use personal trainers?" Do you know what I say to that? "Only those people who are serious about getting results, only the serious ones."

When I instituted this program in my club the impact on my sales was instant. When I created the "training team" concept the paradigm had shifted from "this person is trying to sell me personal training to," "I hope I qualify to be on the training team."

Can you see the difference in the two? People love to qualify for something. Remember how happy you were when you came home from school and told your parents that you made the team (what ever team it was)? There was a sense of accomplishment, and you had a road map set up to help you accomplish that goal.

What about when you didn't make the team? There was devastation, depression, and sometimes embarrassment of having to look at your friends because many of them made the team.

I am going to teach you how people, you and me, have very deep rooted emotions that drive our every step.   When you begin to understand this, you will really begin to understand people. The key here is to always focus what you learn about people, onto your self. "The more you study you, the more you will understand everyone else."

-INCOME GOALS-

When setting up sales goals, I always liked paying more attention to the number of people I brought on to the training team, as opposed to focusing on a certain number of dollars that I needed to reach goal. This made it much more fun to come to the club. Think about it, your goal is to help people get results that will change their lives. When your mind is focused on the money aspect of it, you lose sight of why you are really there. Ask your self this question, "Can I make money without having anyone join the training team?" Well of course not!!

O.K., ask this question, "Can I have people join my training team, and NOT make money?" Impossible! So, you are always killing two birds with one stone if you focus on bringing people to your training team.

My wife would always ask me, "Honey, how big is your check this pay period?" I would always say, "I have no idea." This was always a little irritating for her to hear, but I knew if I just kept focusing on bringing people to my training team, then I would always have money, and honestly, I never added up my check before I received it, so I really didn't know what it was. I just looked at my "year to date" and I knew it was more than anyone else's. People love to complain about how small their checks are. I just listened to them and realized I wasn't in that boat.

Let's look at how you would calculate the number of people you need to satisfy your boss and yourself. I am assuming that you have a weekly, biweekly or monthly goal. Whatever that number is; just take an average size deal and figure out how many people you would have to bring on to the training team in order to reach that number. Simple,

I did it all the time. This technique will allow you to always focus on the "real reason" you are in the fitness business, and still make a bunch of money, far more than you would the other way. Believe me when I say, this method has been tried and tested many, many times. Implement this TODAY!!

Chapter Six
Setting Appointments
Duplicate Yourself

● ●

What is the one thing that all "sales people" either complain about or are nervous about not having?

This would be the ever sought after APPOINTMENTS; people to share their product or service with.

I am going to share with you my N.E.D'S program.

There are three segments of fitness club members:

- New members
- Existing members
- Dead members

The first segment of the member base you want to serve is the new members.

-NEW MEMBERS-

When starting your work day, wouldn't it be nice to have an endless supply of people to share your belief in the value of personal training? Well, of course it would. How many people does your club bring in a month? The clubs I have been in bring in anywhere from 50 to 700 a month.

Whatever the number is, how many do you have an option to have an appointment with the day they join the club, or within a few days after? Let me tell you how many you should be having an appointment with, 95% of them. Nothing in life is 100%, right? Let me share with you how you do this. You create a win-win situation for you and the front desk people. You know, the people that are busy signing people up, making health drinks and simply, or not so simply, running the club. This is a big responsibility. They don't just stand behind the counter and do nothing. There is a series of questions that you need to ask them:

1. "Do you guys (purely slang for people) sign people up to join the club?" Answer, YES!
2. "Do you tell the people they are going to get a free fitness evaluation when they sign up, so they can get started in the right direction?" Answer, YES!
3. "Do the most recent people that you signed up come up to the front counter looking for guidance of some sort?" Answer, YES!
4. "Do you have time to during your busy day; while you are supposed to be signing up new members, to design a program for them, even if it is just a starter program?" Answer, NO!
5. "Do you have a quota or goal you must meet for the number of people you have to sign up each month?" Answer, YES!
6. "Would it help you if I did a fitness evaluation for your new members, and also started them on their first four week program?" Answer, YES!
7. "If I promised that you would never have to worry about ANY members coming up and asking for your assistance with workout schedules, routines, or techniques, as it pertained to reaching their goals, would that be a big help to you?" Answer, YES, YES, AND YES again!!!

"Then all I ask is that you make sure that after you sign the new member up, you put them in my appointment book for their evaluation. This will ensure that no one will slip through the cracks, as far as having no guidance in the beginning. I will get them all started on the right program, and headed in the right direction to ensure their fitness success. If for some reason they are not able to commit to an appointment time right then and there; please, just leave a list of those folks for me on my desk, and I will take care of scheduling them. Sound cool?" Answer, YES!

This strategy is a win-win for everyone involved. You are doing the front counter staff a great service, you are getting your appointment book filled consistently, and the new member is getting their evaluation like they were told they were going to get, and also they are getting a four week starter routine WHETHER THEY SIGN UP FOR PERSONAL TRAINING OR NOT!! This part is the key part to the entire technique, let me explain.

-KEEP MEMBERS WITHIN REACH-

This is vital in order to keep members within your reach. Just because someone doesn't join the training team the first time, doesn't mean they won't join the team at a later date. I have experienced this many times. When you do what is right by people, they generally remember.

First of all, if you didn't sign them up on the training team the first time, then obviously you didn't do a good enough of a job at showing the value of personal training and the training team. Why take it out by shunning them, and making them feel like all you wanted was their money? Put them on a four week program, show them that you really do care about their fitness needs, and then you have a great reason to keep talking to them. It's only a four week program. You and I both know that no matter what program you are on, it only generally lasts four to six weeks before it starts running dry, or will plateau.

Since 42% of all people who join a fitness facility stop actively coming to the club after just 30 days, I think it is obvious what you should do. If the member quits coming to the club after 30 days, then you have a ZERO % chance of getting them to join your training team. If you just help them stay around long enough to finish a four week program, you have a far better chance of getting them on your team. And besides, you look great for doing it. You held up your end of the bargain to the front desk crew; everyone is getting closer by the minute when everyone starts working together. This means everyone wins, and isn't that what everyone is there to do?

Quick example; I did this when I worked in the clubs as a general manager (front line sales or as we know it now as professional communicator). I duplicated myself by six. This means, I had the efforts of six other people helping me set appointments, as well as my self. I always had a full appointment book, and as far as the other 5% of the people that wouldn't commit to an appointment the day they joined the club, this is what I said when I called them,

"Hello Sally, this is Duane from (club name) I do the fitness evaluations for the new members and also help you set up your fitness programs so you can get quicker results than you were probably expecting. Are you coming to the club tomorrow or Thursday (or what ever the next day after tomorrow is)? (Member) tomorrow, (me) good, what time works well for you? I will need about an hour to complete the evaluation."

This is ALL I ever did. I assumed that everyone wanted an evaluation. If you are confident and sure, then people will feel confident and sure. I would spend 20 minutes on the phone setting appointments. I would set five to six appointments in a 20 minute time frame, anytime I wanted. I was NEVER starved for people to be sitting in front of.

The next segment of the member base that you want to serve is the existing members.

-EXISTING MEMBERS-

I explained the important's of existing members earlier in chapter three. It is vital to be a "presence" in your club. We talked about working people out for free. We discussed the value of the "Doctor image" you need to exude. Please review chapter three for more clarity on existing members.

-DEAD MEMBERS-

This segment is very profitable, but often forgotten. Give them a call, get them off the couch. You will be amazed how many people you can get to come back to the club after they have been off for several months, and when you do get them to come back, how hard do you think it is to get them to join you training team? Give me a break, this is ridiculously easy. You're the entire reason they are coming back. You successfully got them off the couch. No small success by any means. This is the 42% that quit the first month because they got frustrated, depressed, and discouraged. You owe it to these members to "dust them off" and give them "renewed" hope in reaching their physical and emotional goals.

Do you want to hear how I got them to come back in? I thought so; this is what I did, "Hello Sally, this is Duane from (club name), it looks like you have been a member here for several months, but it also looks like you haven't worked out here in a while. (Right about now, they will give you a hundred reasons why they haven't came in I never ask them why I just immediately say . . .)

We are running a program where we are calling all our members that "want" or "NEED" to get started back on track to reach their fitness goals, and offering a fitness evaluation, and two free sessions with our training team in order to help you get back on track. Summer is coming up and we are sure you want to look your best. Or, winter is coming up and we are sure you do not want to fall into the couch potato role and gain a bunch of weight due to having no outside activity, then struggle to get it off in the spring time." Obviously pick your season, "all seasons hold reasons for getting in shape." As I always say "there is a reason for every season."

You should never have a shortage of appointments.

Remember the N.E.D.'S:

New members, existing members, and dead members-

Within the N.E.D.'S there is a variety of personality types, and emotions: frustrated members, goal driven members, excited members, or depressed members. They all are candidates for your training team.

Chapter Seven
Expect your results

• •

Before we go any farther, I must talk about the importance of expectation. "It doesn't matter where you are outside; it only matters where you are inside."

These are the most important words you will ever hear. Allow me to explain. No matter how incredible the techniques are that you are going to learn in this book, they will do you absolutely no good if one thing isn't in line,

YOUR EXPECTATION OF YOUR RESULTS.

"NEVER EXPECT SOMETHING YOU DO NOT WANT, AND NEVER WANT SOMETHING YOU DO NOT EXPECT."

I am going to tell you about a situation that I was involved in with a company that opened the eyes of hundreds of people in eight short days. I was looking for a company to perform my magic with. I had emailed one of the owners about the opportunity to put my communication techniques to use in their company. I proceeded to tell the owners that I had a unique way of selling, and that I had invented many years ago. It had served me very well when I was building my own companies. My techniques were unlike anything they had ever seen, I boasted! They were very intrigued, but of course, skeptical. I suggested that they put me in the worst club that they had in the country. Anyone can look good or produce in a good club; put me in the situation that you would consider hopeless, if in fact you have a club like this.

They had what they considered the perfect club for me to try my techniques.

The club was a Gym in Battle Creek, Michigan. They proceeded to tell me that they had gone through seven sales managers in the last ten months. They proceeded to tell me that, not only was the club a mess, but the entire town of Battle creek was the pits. The city was in the top ten percent in many categories that are not conducive to economic success. Unemployment, foreclosure and bankruptcy rates were at the top of the charts. The owners of this company proceeded to tell me that they had really messed this club up. They had put the wrong people in the sales manager position several times, and the members of the club, as well as the working staff were very, very unhappy with the results that they were getting.

Everything that came out of their mouth was extremely negative. They had nothing good to say about ANYTHING to do with this situation. I appreciated their honesty; after all it was refreshing to not have someone feed me a line of crap about how great a situation is, just to walk into a nightmare. I definitely wasn't being painted a pretty picture. The owners proceeded to tell me that although my resume was very impressive, they felt that it would still take me four months to get the club up to the level of their EXPECTATION, which was to sell $15,000 of personal training each pay period, which was every two weeks. Again, I appreciated their candor, but I had other ideas. I told them, "Whatever you guys think is going to happen, I promise you, it is going to be much different than that." I wasn't trying to be cocky, but at the same time, I realize so deeply the "expectation" factor. I had no idea where the club was in Battle Creek. I had been to Battle Creek several times, but I had never seen fitness club there before. It didn't matter to me where the club was. It only mattered to me where "I" was.

This is what happened:

I walked into the club on the fourth of the month. I literally just walked around for four days, meeting people, looking at things, absorbing the entire situation. I was creating pictures in my mind, literally building an "image" of what "I wanted" to see. I was building "brain cells of recognition." All the while, people were coming up to me and saying the craziest stuff, "We hate the company that you work for, they are a lousy company. They have really messed this place up." Then another group of people would say, "I don't know what that personal training company was thinking by coming into this club. There is no money here. People in this town don't have any money."

Well, I would just smile, and keep building the "picture" that I wanted to see. This is the key to the entire thing. I would "choose" to pick out all the good that the club and town had to offer. I found a lot of things to be excited about. First I started with the town. Everyone said that there wasn't any money in this town. No one had any money, yet there were all sorts of business's open; several restaurants, malls, big stores, you know, Lowe's, Home Depot, Menard's, Kohl's, Sam's Club - all the big ones. Where is everyone getting the money to support these mega stores if there isn't any money in this town? I started looking at what kind of cars were in the fitness club's parking lot; there were really nice cars; Mercedes, BMW's, corvettes, and of course, Ford, Chevrolet's, and the like.

Hmm! This wasn't making any sense to me. Then I focused my attention on the club itself. I looked at all the really nice equipment that they had. The club staff was great; Brandlelynn, Rod, Alex, Ethan, Britney, and of course, Richard Baker. Richard was the club manager. Richard was the best manager I ever seen. I don't mean just in the fitness industry, I mean in any industry. I interviewed the personal training staff; I felt I had as good a staff as any club.

Let me fast forward to this - the history of this club, from a personal training stand point, was that of selling $500 to $1000 of personal training in a two week period. Dead last in the country pay period after pay period. This club was the laughing stock of the company. I actually started selling, or as I refer to it, communicating, on the eighth of the month; I only had until the 15th of that month to hit my goal numbers, which I mentioned was $15,000. I also mentioned that the owners of the company I was working for thought it would take me four months to get to the point that I could start to hit the $15,000 goal. Well, let me say this; not only did I shock the company I was working for, I devastated the other 52 fitness clubs that this company was working in. Because within the next seven days I sold $22,500 of personal training out this fitness club in Battle Creek, Michigan. The place where they said it could never be done - from worst to first in seven days-number one in the country!

I was on the national conference call the day after the pay period had ended. I was of course, the topic of conversation. The obvious question was, "How in the world did I you take a perennial loser and turn it into the best club in the country in just seven days?" My answer was simple, "The money that I generated in seven days, was there for the other seven managers to have. I didn't do anything that anyone else couldn't have done." Remember, I was saying that I was "painting the picture" of my EXPECTATION. This is very important to understand. The other seven managers were also painting "their" picture of what they EXPECTED. They looked all around, and found reasons why they couldn't sell personal training in this club. They listened to all the "experts" in the club, and in the town who said, "No one has any money in this town, BLAH, BLAH, and BLAH!! They got so caught up in the "easy way" to think, "Having belief in something that you can see and touch, is no belief at all." I "CHOSE" to expect the good that I desired. The other managers "CHOSE" to expect "what the "experts" told them. We were both right in what we "expected" to happen – my "expectation" just paid better!

They couldn't see past their circumstances. Circumstances, hell, I make them. If the circumstances are not what I want, I will make my own. People that get on in this world have a clear understanding of what I mean by this.

Here is the key to making your own circumstances, "Start thinking about the solution instead of the problem." You can never solve a problem at the level of the problem. You have to step back and see the big picture. You MUST find the good in a situation, there is always some good in everything. This is a Universal law; everything has an equal, but opposite side. The Universe must balance itself out. You must find the smallest amount of good, and then you can get a foot hold from that good, and build from there. The people that bought personal training from me were "lifers" in Battle Creek. What I mean by this is, they hadn't just moved in, these people were here for the other seven managers to attract if they chose to. But, you see, all the other managers could do was attract the people that were vibrating on the same energy level as they were. This is scientific folks; this isn't something out of Star Trek.

You must understand the power of expectation; granted, my technique system is the best in the business, this is for sure. Having said this, I did something in just seven days that all the "experts" from corporate headquarters said would take four months to even think of doing. But hell, at least they thought it could be done in some time frame. Everyone else thought this accomplishment could never be done. From the time standpoint alone, I needed some universal power to pull this off, the Universal Law of Expectation. You can learn more about the power of the Universal Laws in my book "Positive Thinking

Sucks, Internalization rules."

I went on to do phenomenal numbers out of that club for several months. The first two months, I sold $94,500 of personal training. Not bad for a club that averaged about $3,000 for two months. The people that received the personal training in that club were the biggest winners. It was a privilege to be on the fitness club's personal training team.

I must say; my time in Battle Creek was some of the best times I have ever had. The relationships that were developed will last a life time. Richard Baker and the Assistant Manager Rod Taylor were vital in my success; as was the head of my personal training department Tanya Marshall-Farnham. Tanya is a phenomenal talent who made it easy for me to be the best I could be. And if I ever needed a good laugh; my buddy Keith Hendrix was always there. Keith was also an incredible trainer. Between Keith and Tonya, we would have so much fun laughing together, that our guts would hurt. These are the kind of times that I will remember forever. These are the kinds of times that the other managers could have had, if they were not so intent on seeing what they COULDN'T do.

Life is truly what you make it. I know that sounds like a cute saying, but when you understand the impact of those words, you will be free to accomplish anything in life that you want to.

Chapter Eight
Open Three Doors to Close One

Now, we are getting to the good stuff, you know, the techniques that are instantly going to make your income at least triple. Like any good system, you must first have a larger view of the picture or situation at hand. This is why I spent a fair amount of time informing you on the mentality you must have in order to maximize your results. I will say this again, I do not want this system to work for anyone that is of the shady nature. These techniques are so valuable, that the opportunity to take advantage of people is certainly there. Since I am assuming that those still reading this book are good people- we will continue on to some income changing techniques, let's go!!

-RELAX AND RELATE-

DOOR NUMBER ONE: People buy from people who they like. As I said, "People do not care how much you know, until they know how much you care." Opening this door will allow you to relax people. You relax people by being able to relate to them. People love to be around people of "like kind," when ever we go ANYWHERE, we are always looking for people that we fit in with. When relaxing someone, you must find some common ground to relate to: kids, sports, hobbies, acquaintances, interests, or any similarities you can find at all. People need to view you as a "real person," not a "sales person." The funny thing is; we know this instinctively, but knowing this is one thing, knowing how to do this is another thing.

Let me give you one hint on what to do - SHUT UP, SHUT UP, AND WHEN YOU HAVE MASTERED THAT - SHUT UP SOME

MORE!!!

"God gave us two ears and one mouth so we can listen twice as much as we talk." Relating to people has NOTHING to do with you. It has everything to do with THEM. What is the number one thing people like to talk about? The answer is, THEMSELVES. Your job is to get people to talk about the topics of interest, which you both may or may not have in common. I promise you this, if someone talks long enough on any topic, you will be able to relate to something that they are speaking about. I have listened to people for hours and talked for maybe 15 minutes during the entire time. Later, I run into people that know this person and they say, "Hey Duane, I hear you talked a couple hours with Joe. He said you were a great guy. He loved talking with you the other day." Joe loved talking to me because I let him talk about himself. This is a very, very crucial part of communicating this, "RELAXING AND RELATING."

I have sat with sales people while critiquing their sales techniques, and I would was flabbergasted at the amount of talking they were doing during the conversation. They would be done with their presentation, and ask me what I thought. I would ask them some very simple questions:

"Do you know what their kids' names are?"

"Do you know how old their kids' are?"

"Do you know what their kids' favorite hobbies are?"

"Do you know what their spouses name is?"

"Do you know what their spouses' hobbies are?"

"Do you know the "real reason" joined this club?"

AND ON AND ON AND ON WE GO!! I could have listed another 20 things. You should know everything about this person before you are through. This is what allows people to "relax and relate" to you, not a bunch of crap about your product or service; boring, boring, boring.

You will need all of this information that your client is talking about. You will utilize this information within your presentation. Look at it this way, "if you talk long enough, I will figure out exactly how to sell you." Now, I know this sounds a little cold. I really do need to know what "value" you are putting on personal training. I can only know this, however, if I know what you're hot or emotional buttons are. This takes an immense amount of information gathering, and you will only share the really deep rooted good stuff with me if you are RELAXED. You will have the opportunity to do your dog and pony show, you know, show all the cool stuff about your personal training program. Please, do not get me wrong, the nuts and bolts of what you offer are very important BUT, not at the expense of really getting to know your client and having them "feel" that you can "RELAX AND RELATE" to them.

Now that I have made it clear on the importance of letting your client do the majority of the talking. As we get further into the techniques, I will show you how you can talk a little more than usual during the "relating" phase. I will give you a hint; the relating portion will be used in the dog and pony part of your presentation. You will have the opportunity to talk about how all of our bodies relate to each other, to a large degree. This is a fun "relating" time that makes your client realize that we are all very much alike in many physical ways; this brings comfort to your client.

-DESIRE AND DISTURB-

DOOR NUMBER TWO: Once you have gathered a lot of information from your client during the "relax and relate" phase, you are now ready to open the next important door. You will certainly have enough information to open this door and organize a flow of questioning that will allow them to talk about the real deep reasons for their DESIRE to get fit.

"Joe, you told me that your parents died young. Is this something that scares you and you wanted to prevent it from happening to you?"

"Joe, you told me that you have wanted to get back to the way you use to look and feel. You have been terribly depressed since you have been out of shape. Joe, are you ready to cure that depression and feel great again?"

"Sally, you said that you are really sick and tired of shopping in the "big women's" stores. It makes you feel rejected by society. Sally would you like to shop in the normal stores so you can feel good about fitting in with mainstream society?"

"Sally, you said that there is a lot of diabetes in your family, and if you continue to gain any more weight, your doctor said that you will be at a very high risk for the disease. Sally, would you like to make sure you are healthy so you can raise your daughter Elizabeth and really enjoy her formidable years?"

"Joe, you said you are in the white collar business sector, and since you are in your mid-forties now you feel that you need to be able to keep up with all the younger people that are vying for your job. Joe, would you like to give yourself a better opportunity for job security by being in your the best possible shape? As they say, "This is a young mans world!"

"Sally, you said that your husband Bill doesn't seem to pay as much attention to you as he used to. The romantic times are few and far between. Sally would you like to have that passion back in your marriage?"

These reasons are "THE REASONS" why they will join your training team, NOT the dog and pony show, or nuts and bolts of the "cool" equipment. I do not care how much great information you have on personal training. All the statistics, all the facts and figures, all the things that make "perfect sense" to you, as to why your client needs personal training; THE MAJORITY of people will NOT join your training team for those reasons – those are your reasons, not theirs - PERIOD!!!!

When you rely on the technical information to sell your client, you are setting yourself up for about a 20% closing percentage. By using this method the number of people that you are NOT getting to join you team is IMMENSE. "Facts and figures make you think; emotion makes you act." I am going to go into this much more as we get to the 12 step techniques later in this lesson.

Once you have firmly solidified the DESIRE to join the training team, the next very important thing to do is DISTURB the desires.

"Fear of loss is the greatest motivator to man."

When we get our thought process or mind made up about something that really means a lot to us, we do not want to let go of it. This is what I would say when I wanted to see if my clients were really ready to do what ever it took to reach their "DESIRES;" I would ask, "Sally, you really have convinced me that your desires are very important to you. What would happen if you didn't get your desires? What would happen if they never came true?" The fear in most people's eyes when I ask this- is nothing short of frightful. The thought of not being able to have these desires in their life is almost more than they can bear. When your client lets' you know the importance of their desires, then you go to the next door.

-SOLUTION-

DOOR NUMBER THREE:

Opening this door allows you to share with your client the great opportunity that you have for them to reach their goals, so they can have their desires. At this point, you are really just reviewing with them the relating part of the process. Remember, I said that you will be able to present to them the "dog and pony show" part of your presentation during the relating stage.

Lets' make sure we understand what the "dog and pony" show is. This is where you will educate your client on how the human body works in the respect of body metabolism, muscle burns fat, caloric intake and burning, workout plateau, resistance training, and cardio target heart rate, etc., etc., etc. Your client will have a full understanding of what you offer in the form of personal training. What the solution step will do is tie together for them the dog and pony show and the VALUE it has for them. The lights click on at this point; you have the vehicle that will deliver to them the desires of their heart. The VALUE of personal training has now come full circle. The thought of personal training is NO LONGER related to spending money, working out, sweating, having sore muscles, being inconvenienced, or having another "task" that NEEDS to be completed today!! NO, NO, NO, personal training is thought of as THE PROCESS that will fill my EMOTIONAL, MENTAL, AND PHYSICAL NEEDS. This is what will get your closing percentage doubled, tripled, and even quadrupled; thus doubling, tripling, and quadrupling your income-GUARANTEED!!!

-CLOSE-

DOOR NUMBER FOUR:

Door number four is the only door that you do not open, you close it; as in "close the deal." This is the biggest misnomer in the sales industry. Sales people seem to think that they have to be great closers. Well, I guess if you are selling in the normal sense you would. I do not sell, I COMMUNICATE. I teach people to be MASTER COMMU-

NICATORS not low life sales people. This is as clear as I can make it; SALES PEOPLE CARE ABOUT THEMSELVES; COMMUNICATORS CARE ABOUT OTHER PEOPLE. You cannot possibly communicate with people correctly and not care about them, and you cannot "sell" to people and care about them at all. This is why, when you communicate with people, you have to listen intently, and if you are a "sales" person, you generally do not have the patience to listen intently, because you're too concerned with making the "sale" so you can get out of there and go make another "sale."

The irony is that you will make a heck of a lot more "sales" if you just relax, and care enough about people that you have the patience to communicate with them. This takes LISTENING; listening is something a "sale person" is terrible at doing.

This four door format is intended to lay the foundation of the 12 steps that we are going to go into in a short while. This 12 step system has been perfected over many years, and implemented all across the country. From the moment you shake your prospective client's hand coming in your door, to the handshake while leaving your door, my system will walk you through the step by step process to doubling, tripling, and quadrupling your income.

Chapter Nine
Psychology of Persuasion

I would like to talk to you about some persuasion techniques that are going to become extremely important when going through the 12 step system. As you will see, the art of persuasion is an incredible asset to have. This is why I am so intent on NOT teaching my system to anyone that would abuse the privilege of learning it.

The following chapter will cover a lot of information, that you would do yourself great justice in learning, and more importantly APPLYING. I am going to go in depth into just a portion of it. The portion, I believe is extremely vital to your success in the fitness industry as a PROFESSIONAL COMMUNICATOR.

Let's go!!!

> "The ability to deal with people is as purchasable a commodity as sugar or coffee. I will pay more for that ability, than for any other under the sun."
> - John D. Rockefeller

> "If there is any one secret of success, it lies in the ability to get the other person's point of view and see things from his angle."
> - Henry Ford

> "Opinion is ultimately determined by feelings, not by intellect."
> - Herbert Spencer

> "If you would win a man to your cause, first convince him that you are his sincere friend."
> - Abraham Lincoln

"The only way on earth to influence the other fellow is to talk about what he wants and show him how to get it."
- Dale Carnegie

"You can make more friends in two months by becoming interested in other people, than you can in two years trying to get other people interested in you."
- Dale Carnegie

"Action springs out of what we fundamentally desire."
- Prof. Harry A. Overstreet
Influencing Human Behavior

"First arouse in the other person an eager want. He who can do this has the whole World with him. He who cannot, walks a lonely way."
-Prof. Harry A. Overstreet

"People get a feeling, and then they purchase the feeling."
- Duane L. McGill

Human Behavior Sales Academy

The definition of persuasion is the ability to induce beliefs and values in other people by influencing their thoughts and actions through specific strategies. Psychology in its most literal definition is the study of the soul, the soul meaning the true individual.

Much of the information from this chapter is from the book "The Psychology of Persuasion," by Kevin Hogan.

I do not want to mislead you in thinking that I invented this material, anymore than Kevin would want you to think he did. Great teachers gather information from various sources, and then distribute the information to their students. The book "The Psychology of Persuasion" is such a phenomenal book; I see no reason to "re-package" this material. I strongly suggest you to get this book, so you can further your education on some very important topics.

I will enlighten you on many areas of the "Psychology of persuasion." I will relate this information to the fitness Industry so you can have an excellent example of how to implement it in a way that will bring "value" to your career as a health and fitness professional.

READ, READ, READ

We are all motivated towards "pleasure" or away from "pain." All of our behavior comes down to choosing or responding to various forms of stimulus that takes us toward our goals or moves us away from our fears. Let's dig into this a little farther.

Example: if one of your prospective clients is a lady that is 50 lbs. over weight, and has always been 50 lbs. over weight; what direction do you think she is going in? Is she motivated towards pleasure or trying to get away from pain? Let's consider this-when a person has always been heavy, by our standards, we can be fairly sure that they have probably been looked at, or possibly treated rudely at some point in their lives, just because of their weight issue. I know this sucks, but this is a fact in our judgmental society. Would it be a good idea to talk to this lady about getting excited about wearing a size three outfit? This lady probably hasn't been in a size three since she was a very young girl, if ever at all! This is the lady that I gave an example of several pages back, when I said, "Sally was tired of shopping at the big women's store."
If you were to ask her this question, you would find out really quick which way she is going. This is the question, "Sally, if you lived on a desert island all by your self, with all the amenities that you would ever need, would it matter if you lost 50 lbs.?" The answer will generally be NO!!

You see, Sally isn't concerned with going towards the pleasure of the size three outfits, because Sally isn't "mentally wired" to have the picture in her mind of what a size three feels like. A size three isn't a really believable option. Please, do not misunderstand me. I am the kind of person that believes ANYTHING is possible; so the fact that Sally doesn't believe this doesn't mean my opinion reflects that belief. Sally is more inclined to be trying to remove herself from the pain of social scrutiny, not trying to look like the Baywatch girls. Sally's vision of success is walking into a restaurant without being looked at in disgrace, or being able to bypass the big women's store and shop with the rest of "accepted" society. If you start communicating with Sally on the level of pleasure instead of pain, you will probably be wondering why Sally needs to join the training team, but she just doesn't join.

How about the lady that was always thin in high school or college? You know-the cheerleader or athletic type that was always praised for how good she looked. Now she is middle aged, 50 lbs. over weight, has three kids, and a sit-down career. This lady, we will call her Beth. She obviously wants to get back to the younger Beth. She realizes exactly what it feels like to be in a size three outfit. Beth is the kind of women, that if you ask her about the island with no one on it, and all the amenities she could ask for she would say, "I don't care if anyone is on this island or not; I am going to shed this 50 lbs. if it kills me; I want my younger body again, or as close to it as I can." Beth is "mentally wired" to have a clear understanding of the "feeling" of being fit, and this is not necessarily dependent on what anyone else thinks. You can paint Beth the picture of the pleasure of getting back in shape all you want to, she will eat it up. She will be thinking- been there, done that!!

Do not get these two examples twisted around, it will cost you dearly in your pocket book, GUARANTEED!!

READ, VERY GOOD TO UNDERSTAND

1. Nine Laws of persuasion:
   A. Reciprocity (Put a mini-refrigerator in your office, workout client more than once. Offer them juice, water, protein drinks, etc.)
   B. Contrast (Show the client the difference between your training team and their own training.)
   C. Friend (When someone asks you to do something, and you perceive that person to have your best interest in mind, you are strongly motivated to fulfill their request. You will build value in the "training team"- your client will know that their "friend" thinks it is best for them to choose to join the training team)
   D. Expectancy (When someone you believe in or respect expects you to buy, you will tend to fulfill their expectation. Your client will know that if they "expect" to accomplish their goals – you would "expect them to join the training team)
   E. Association (We tend to like services that are endorsed by people we respect or like. This can include World class athletes who have personal trainers, or other people in your own fitness club)
   F. Consistency (Yes, I had a great workout. Yes, I believe personal training will help me. Yes, I want to get in the best shape of my life, etc.)
   G. Scarcity (I cannot guarantee these prices beyond today. Our best trainers' schedules are filling up quick, etc.)
   H. Conformity (People like being involved with the majority of the population, involved with the group. "Do a lot of people have personal trainers?" "Only the people that are serious about their fitness goals like you are Sally.")
   I. Power (You have power over people when you have greater

strength, authority, and expertise. There are more followers in this World than there are leaders. You offer a great service – lead people to it!)

2. O.B.T. Outcome based thinking is the ability to "visualize" the precise outcome of a process before beginning that process:

   A. What precisely do I want out of the process?
   B. What does the other person want?
   C. What is the least I will accept out of the process?
   D. What problems could come up in the process?
   E. How will I deal with each one, and if possible, use the problem as a benefit?
   F. How will I bring the process to a conclusion?

We discussed the topic of "expectation" in chapter seven. We also discussed the "open three doors to close one" in chapter eight. O.B.T is an outline, or checklist that you want to keep in mind, as you are conducting your "fitness evaluation." The 12 step method will ensure that all these areas are accounted for.

THE MOST IMPORTANT TOPIC TO REMEMBER

3. What are the two most motivating feelings? - Pleasure and Pain. We discussed this in the beginning of this chapter. All of your "communicative skills" should be built around the "pleasure" – "pain" concept.

THE FORMAT FOR YOUR ENTIRE PRESENTATION

4. The four sections to a presentation:
   A. Relax and Relate
   B. Desire and Disturb

C. Solution

D. Close

NEVER, EVER, present this list "out of order."

READ, READ, READ

5. Communication: content of information 7%; voice tone, fluctuation, and physiology 38%; painting a picture of feeling 55%. We covered a part of this briefly in our four door section. Remember, I was saying that you need to listen, listen, and listen some more.

You see, only 7% of what you are talking about; meaning the "content" of your presentation (the dog and pony show), has anything to do with your client's decision to purchase your personal training service. So, why would you talk 80% of the time?

38% of the decision making process involves voice tone, fluctuation, and physiology. We can see this being very true; think about the music you listen to. Think about how you are attracted to certain voice tones on answering machines or other "voice only" devices. Also, your physical appearance is very important; you obviously need to be well groomed.

55% of the reason people decide to purchase your personal training is obviously the "feeling" that you are able to help them "visualize"- this is the main reason for any purchase. Of course you do need to present properly; thus the other 45% of the determining factor. If you had to go in the presentation with only one thing, you better be the master of creating a "feeling."

READ, READ

6. Mirroring: You move how they move. People like to be around

people that they view as themselves. Mirroring the other person's body gives them a sense of similarity. They subconsciously feel "oneness" with you without even knowing why. When you are sitting with your client, be VERY conscious of this fact.

READ

7. Best time to smile: beginning, middle optional, and end. (Shows you are friendly but serious, and focused on their situation. When giving your client an evaluation, the "balance" must be precise.)

READ, READ, READ

8. BIG TIME IMPORTANT: colors will make your job much, much easier. We will go more in depth in the "ambiance" section of this book.

Powerful colors for maximizing the mood for buying personal training:

BLUE - Is the No. 1 communicating color and dreaming color. When should this be used? Answer: write down goals and values on blue paper during evaluation.

RED – No. 1 selling and passion color. When should this be used? Write down goals and values with red marker, on blue paper, during evaluation.

LIGHT BROWN - Relaxing and affordable color. When should this be used? Tables and walls should be light brown.

PASTELS - Relaxing color. When should this be used? Pictures should have pastel coloring.

BLACK AND WHITE - sterile and doctor colors. When should this be used? It should be used ONLY when presenting page one and page two of evaluation. (The prescription: just what the doctor ordered!)

YELLOW – No. 1 color that the retina sees first. If yellow is in the room, your eyes will go to it first. When should this be used? ALL employees, at the field level, should have 'trainer' written in yellow on the back of their shirts. Subliminally, patrons of the club will look at the word dozens more times than they do now while they are in the clubs. Patrons of the club will develop, at least an urge, to talk to a trainer about tips and fitness programs.

READ, READ

9. Proximity- The comfortable distance between yourself and your client. This is very important to make sure people are at a comfort able physical distance. The more comfortable the distance, the more attention they have on getting the feeling for personal training.
   A. Men influencing men- 3 to 6 feet apart.
   B. Men influencing women- 2 to 8 feet, depending on feedback.
   C. Women influencing men- 1.5 to 4 feet.
   D. Women influencing women- 1.5 to 4 feet.

READ, READ, READ

10. Round Table - 90 degree angle when setting with client. Definitely DO NOT SIT ACROSS from anyone that you are communicating with, unless it's someone else's attorney or your ex-spouse! This is a very combative position that will pit you against them.

You want to have a friendly, "we are working on this project together" atmosphere. This is done when you and the other person is either side by side or at a 90 degree angle. This makes all the difference in the world to the comfort level of your client during their evaluation.

REVIEW AND VISUALIZE THIS STEP

11. Touching- Proper areas of touching a client, for comfort as well as psychological advantage:
    A. Men to men- hand, shoulder, forearm, upper arm.
    B. Men to women- hands, forearm
    C. Women to women- hand, forearm, upper arm, knee
    D. Women to men- entire body (within reason)

Non-verbal bad cues-
    E. Hand and fingers' to nose and mouth.
    F. Arms crossed
    G. Eye contact

Visualize the obvious areas of your client's body that you should touch during their evaluation. I think you will find this easy to implement.

READ, READ, READ

12. What is a persons' favorite thing to hear? - Their name. I cannot stress this enough. The attention of your client will go through the roof the more you say their first name. We LOVE to hear our first name. You should say your client's first name before or after every sentence. You will mesmerize them with this technique. If you want your client's FULL ATTENTION, then this is an

absolute must.

READ, READ, READ

13. Power words- name, please, thank you, and because are the four best. Other good power words: save, advantage, guarantee, happy, results, value, exciting, deserve, fun, vital. We are mentally programmed to respond to these power words. Do you ever wonder why commercials use them all the time?

I DON'T THINK I HAVE TO EXPLAIN THE NO. 14 AND 15, VERY WELL COVERED.

14. Who should be talking more, you or the client?
Answer – Client!

15. What is a persons' favorite thing to talk about?
Answer – themselves!

Think about this, how often do you have the chance to express your "inner most dominant" feelings? If you are like most people, you may only done this a handful of times your entire life – if at all. The fitness evaluation allows your client to express their feelings. This is very invigorating for them, and very vital to your success of helping them "commit" to their health and fitness goals.

READ, READ, READ

16. Means values and end values, what does this mean? Answer - The means value is the personal training. The end value is the feeling the client receives from the training. Which one do you think is going to sell the personal training to the client? We dis-

cussed this a few pages back. Example: in the "Sally" example we used earlier. Joining the training team is the "means" value, the vehicle Sally needed to get to her desired goal. Her goal was to get away from the pain of societies criticism. The "end" value would be the actual result of succeeding at getting away from that criticism. Another example: "Means value," Joe buys a new Corvette for himself when he turns 50 years old. The "end value" is that Joe bought the corvette because he wanted a certain "feeling" from driving the corvette. Joe wanted to "feel" accomplished, relive some of his youth. Joe also wanted to "feel" as though he could compete with the younger guys for the pretty girls. Joe needed a "means" to get to the "end." This is why you need to find out WHAT THE "END VALUE" IS FOR YOUR CLIENT. This is the information that is going to take your closing percentage from 20% to 80% in a matter of minutes from the time you apply this technique.

I have sat with hundreds of people across the country and showed them how to do this technique. Within minutes of their client walking through the door, and during that first presentation of JUST learning this technique, they were able to close deals that they otherwise had no way of closing. These are their words, not mine.

VERY, VERY IMPORTANT; WE HAVE CLEARLY DISCUSSED THIS.

17. "People don't care how much you know, until they know how much you care."

People get "jacked" around almost every day by people looking to take advantage of them. It is critical that your client feels your sincerity.

READ, READ, READ;
CLEARLY UNDERSTAND THIS VALUE

18. Value system of client. "If we do not clearly know what the values of our clients are, we will assign our own values to the people we communicate with." By now you should have a clear understanding of the importance of your client's value system. As I stated earlier with the "Sally" situation; you need to find out what "value" Sally gave to joining your training team. Your "value" of the training team doesn't matter; Sally's "value" is what is going to make her commit to her goals. DO NOT GET THIS MIXED UP. You like certain music for a reason. Someone else may like the same music, but for entirely different reasons. If you are going to sell them this music you better communicate to them on the level of their "value" of the music.

19. Confide in people, you will tend to get reciprocal behavior. People like to know that you are "real" There is a fine line here, but it's very important that your client knows that you "understand" where they are coming from.

20. Future pacing- "When you get your fitness results, will you stay with us in the future?"
Simply ASSUME your client has already joined your training team.

READ, READ, READ
SUPER VALUABLE-SUPER IMPORTANT

21. Personality types - visual, auditory, kinesthetic, auditory

digital. There many explanations of personality type. One expert will call a personality type one name, and another expert will refer to the same personality type by a different name. For the sake of our conversation I am going to explain, in very simple form, four personality types that are easy to understand.

Visual - most people are this personality type. You can tell this person because they will always talk in terms of things look good, I like what I see, I will see you later.

How to tell when someone is "visual" during your presentation: They will always be looking at the paperwork you are showing them, often, even when you are looking at them while speaking.

Auditory - Many people are auditory communicators. This person listens to everything you say; "I hear that," I like what I am hearing," "I will talk to you later."

How to tell this person is auditory during your presentation: They will always be looking at you even though you are writing or showing them something on paper. If you look up at them, they will be looking right at you mouth. They can actually hear you better by watching your lips move, not unlike the hearing impaired.

Kinesthetic – About 30% of people are kinesthetic. If you just mastered this type, and you currently have a 20% closing percentage, this would raise it to a 50% closing percentage. This is my favorite personality type. When I teach people to communicate correctly with this type, the results are dramatic. Most sales people are of the visual variety. The visual person is really the polar opposite of the kinesthetic. This is why most sales people get very frustrated with this person; they say things like "that person was weird." "They weren't saying anything, they just looked at me." "Why couldn't I get a response out of them?" Well, actually these people are listening and watching you more than any other personality type. This type of person really needs to feel comfortable with you. If you start to talk too fast or get too excited, their eyes will start to flutter.

Have you ever driven down the road about 60 miles an hour and stuck your head out the window? Isn't it difficult to keep your eyes open? You start to squint, don't you? This is exactly what a kinesthetic person feels like when you are talking really fast or getting too excited. They feel the pressure of your personality. They are as irritated or frustrated with you as you are with them.

How to recognize a kinesthetic person:

    A. They will be walking very slowly,

    B. They will talk slower than most people,

    C. They will let you talk a lot,

    D. They will be gathering information to see how they FEEL about that information,

    E. They will be looking around the room trying to FEEL comfortable in their surroundings.

What should you do to communicate with this type? You have to talk slow, move the paperwork around in a slower fashion than normal, and really show them that you care. Never, ever walk ahead of them while you are taking them through a workout. Always walk right next to them at their pace; otherwise they will feel abandoned by you. Kinesthetic people are very sensitive. When kinesthetic people talk, you will want to listen very close because even though they appear to be a little dense, trust me, this is just the opposite of their intellectual program. They process information so slow, that when they do speak, the information has been well thought out, and you can learn a lot from them. The proper touching techniques that we have covered really are very important; this is very important to help us bond with them.

Auditory digital - This is another fun personality type. There are not too many of these people, but they are definitely out there. Boy, can you really blow this sale if you do not know that you are in front of one.

Example: "Hey Frank, what time is it?" "It is 8:32" "Hey Frank, how much is your car payment?" "It is $376.18 cents."

This person is the technical person that HAS to have precise information.

This person is the one that reads every single word on a contract, or sticker on a car window.

This person wants as much literature as you can possibly give them; and they read ALL OF IT!!

This person will NOT make a rash decision on anything; if you gave this person a million dollars in cash; they will have to go home and "think about" whether there is sufficient room in the closet for that much stuff!

O. K., maybe I got a little carried away with that example. This person will normally never buy during the day of exposure to a product or service. If you push them at all, they will leave and NEVER come back. On the other hand, when they make a decision to join your training team, they are in for the long haul. No one will talk them out of it. No three day rescission here!

Key points to cover during your presentation:

Always use exact numbers; example; "Frank, we are going to help you lose 2.3 % body fat in the next 12 days." Do not round up or down. Odd numbers look like you really put a lot of time in figuring out the formula. Auditory digital people love numbers that are exact and precise.

The value in understanding these personality types WILL be the difference between a $30,000 and $100,000 income.

This is what I meant when I said, "You wouldn't wonder why you couldn't COMMUNICATE with someone that speaks another language, if you couldn't speak their language, right?" Well, the "language" of a visual person is FAR different from that of a kinesthetic person. Yes, they are both speaking English, but entirely different varieties of English. You know the term, "there is more than one way to skin a deer," well, there is more than one way to communicate a given language. I strongly encourage you to become a professional at identifying personalities. It pays very, very well.

READ, READ, READ
HYPNOTIC LANGUAGE PATTERNS

This is a great way to point someone in a direction without them realizing you are doing. People generally like to think they are making their own decisions. Hypnotic language patterns are a great way to help them make their own decisions. Remember, when your mom or dad would say, "You know Tom; you may want to get the lawn mowed before it gets dark!" Now you know what they really meant- "Tom get off your butt and get the lawn mowed before it gets too dark, then another day will have gone by, and the grass is going to start looking like crap!" WOW, what a difference! Your parents were trying to tell you, in a very nice way, the repercussions of the lawn not getting mowed. Hypnotic language is an awesome technique to use in the fitness center. Example: when you are out on the floor servicing the members as you should be; as you leave, from showing them a really neat way to train biceps, what you want to say is, "You know Beth, you MAY want to CONSIDER joining the training team." Both of these words are hypnotic language words that will get the member thinking about whether they want to join the training team. Now, if you said to them, "Beth, you should join our training team because we can really help you."

As odd as this may sound; Beth will be far more apt to really consider what the training team can do for her IF she is being asked to consider the option, as opposed to being told she needs to join.

Really study these patterns as often as possible. They can hypnotically help people see the value of your service through the "art" of properly COMMUNICATING.

Hypnotic Language Patterns-
- (Might- Maybe) "You might want to consider a trainer."
- "Maybe you will make the right decision for your fitness goals."
- "(You probably) already know how much better you will feel."
- "(People can, you know) lose weight with our plan."
- "(You will soon realize) how smart you were to get training."
- "(Eventually) you will know this is right for you."
- "(I wouldn't tell you) that you will benefit from our training (because) you already know".
- "(I could tell you) that it is going to be tough to get results on your own, (but I won't)."
- Secrets, everyone feels special when they are told a secret. ("I shouldn't tell you this but...")
- "(Don't feel) as though you have to buy today."

Understand this: Our subconscious mind doesn't "recognize" "don't" and "never." When you say "don't be lazy"- your subconscious mind processes this as "be lazy."

Have you ever wondered why your kids "don't" respond to "don't be lazy," or "don't make a mess." Their subconscious mind has been

processing "be lazy," and "make a mess."
JUST SOMETHING TO THINK ABOUT!!

READ

22. What tone of voice should you use when asking for the sale? Use a lower voice when asking for the sale. Excitable voices during this time are looked at as less of an authority figure voice. Bring your Barry White voice, not your Pee Wee Herman.

READ, WE WILL COVER THIS IN DEPTH IN THE 12 STEP CHAPTERS.

22. What should you have on the table when ending your evaluation? Have absolutely nothing on the table other than the "blue feeling" sheet of paper. You want your client's full attention on their "feeling" for joining your training team. Again, we will cover this in a very short while.

READ, READ

23. What takes more skill and has a much higher closing percentage, hard close or soft close? If you have to hard close your client, you obviously have no real skill as a COMMUNICATOR. I liken a hard closer to a boxer who can only win if he is knocking the other person out. He has no real skill; he has a sluggers chance to win, and that's always a small chance. Just as is the hard closing techniques that unskilled sales people use. This is why they have such low closing percentages and have a terrible referral base. They are always starting fresh every day, because they're so called system isn't conducive to referrals coming from the client's that they had to

hard close. People will not send you their family and friends; just so they can get verbally "beat up." The "close" should be so silent that it doesn't even seem like it is happening. You did exactly what you should have done in COMMUNICATING the value of your personal training service, to show your client the value that it will bring to their lives. This has nothing to do with "slick one liner's" at the closing table to "save a deal."

That was sales people talk. Disgusting isn't it?

As I stated in the beginning of this chapter:

I would like to thank Kevin Hogan for the phenomenal information that I received from his book "The Psychology of Persuasion."

Much of the information in chapter nine came from Kevin's book. I tailored much of the information to make it user friendly for the Person Training Industry.

Chapter Ten
Ambiance of your Room

Setting up your room is a major part of your success. It relieves so much pressure off of you to get them in the mood. Allow me to explain.

It's Valentines Day. You and your wife are going to have a very nice night at home; no kids, just you and her. Now, if you celebrate Valentines Day like most people; it is a romantic experience. Well, imagine when you returned home from work, you walked up to the door, and you were all excited to have a very intimate evening. You opened the door, the kids are screaming, every light in the house is on, the house is a mess, and the television is blaring! How good does your wife have to look, as far as dressed for the evening? You know: sexy red outfit, perfume, hair done up real nice, etc., probably pretty good-right? I mean, the pressure for her to look her best is quite heavy at this point. She has to "make up" for the lack of "mood setting." The ambiance of the room is not conducive to a romantic evening. It is conducive with confusion, disarray, and obnoxious noise. But, what if you returned home, walked up to the house, opened the door, and the room was dimly lit with romantic lighting, the candles were illuminating off the walls and there was romantic music on? How gussied up would your wife have to be now? Heck, she could be wearing a gunny sack at this point. There is no pressure for her to have to "pick up the slack" for a lack of "setting the mood."

Why wouldn't you want to maximize the setting of your office so you can take advantage of the psychological benefits that colors and shapes offer? Let me explain. We have an innate feeling when certain colors and shapes are around us. Night clubs know this; thus strobe lighting. Go to a concert and see the spectacle of colors, or go to a "fire works" show. Let's look at some more subtle examples- watch infomercials. Notice how many light blue shirts you see – remember Billy Mays? Oxyclean!

Go to a bank and notice the dark rich mahogany furniture. The point is this: colors make us feel certain ways. Your office walls and your desk should be beige or light brown. These colors are considered comfortable colors as well as affordable colors. You want your office to be comfortable and also, you want to exude a sense of affordability to your client.

How many times have you walked into a building, you know one of those really expensive looking banks, and you said to yourself, "WOW, this place is beautiful, that desk must have cost a fortune?" Why would you want your clients mind programmed to be thinking about really expensive stuff, when you are trying to convey to them how "affordable" you're personal training is? If we sat a dark mahogany "looking" desk next to a country and western light brown desk; which one would look more expensive? Of course, the mahogany one would. Believe me, you do not want your client looking at the desk where the price sheet is, and thinking about anything expensive. This is very subliminal, but oh, so important.

Let's look at what color the "facts and figure" papers should look like; you know the papers; the dog and pony show part of the presentation. These should be white with black ink. These are considered sterile colors; you know, like doctor office stuff.

This information is serious and informing. This is a good mix to have in this area. There is nothing emotional or exciting about burning calories, or tearing down muscle fibers. These colors will keep the clients attention where it should be.

What about when you get to the part of the presentation where you are discussing your client's values, emotions, and the downright "real" reasons why they are considering joining your personal training team? This part will make or break your closing percentage. Your paper should be one color and your pen should be another color. This is the colors they should be- light blue paper: light blue is a dream color and also a COMMUNICATING color, WOW! Is this ever cool; you are discussing the most important reason why your client is going to join your training team; their deepest desires, passions, and goals, and you're writing it down on a color that is a dream color. Have you ever looked up at a beautiful blue sky and just been caught up in a daze- just dreaming away- thinking of all that you want out of life? Now, imagine sitting with someone and really getting emotional about your dreams and desires. I can absolutely guarantee that your client will not move their eyes off that blue paper. They will be mesmerized and fixated on their desires. I have had many people take that blue paper home with them and tape it to their refrigerator, and also put it on their mirror in the bathroom. This blue paper acts like a crystal ball to the person. Your entire goal is to COMMUNICATE and get your client to dream- this color is magical. When you understand how "feelings" affect your "actions," you will have a clear understanding of why this blue paper is so important. It literally moves people to action- the thinking is done!

Remember what I said, "Facts and figures make us think, but emotion makes us act?" When you see the impact that this technique has on your client, you will never look at light blue paper the same again. Please, understand that the paper MUST be light blue, NOT dark blue. Dark blue is a power color: state police, business CEO's, and Navy officers. All these people wear dark blue. This is a sign of authority and power. This is the total opposite ambiance of what you are trying to convey.

What color is the pen we use when bringing to "life" your client's desires, dreams, and goals? Red-oh yes, this color really brings to life the dreams of your heart. When you are gazing at the sky, or mesmerized by your desires that are written on a light blue sheet of paper, aren't you getting filled with a sense of emotional passion? Sure you are. Well, red is the number one passion color in the world. If you don't think so, just look at Valentine's Day, or go into Victoria's Secret and see what the dominate color is. Red is also the most purchased color in the world. RED MAKES US BUY. We definitely take our wallet out for the color red more than any color invented.

So now, we have our client mesmerized by their desires on light blue paper, and we are writing them down in red, the number one passion color in the world, and also the number one color that makes people purchase whatever is in front of them. When I developed this system, many years ago, I was mesmerized myself on how well it worked. You will just sit back and shake your head when you see what I mean.

Another color of note:

Yellow: canary yellow, WOW, you have to love this color. Actually yellow is the number one color that your retina reacts to first. If you walk into a room, and all colors are equal, your retina will pick up the color yellow first. You really didn't think McDonald's put that big yellow M, or so called the "golden arches" in the sky about 100 ft., by accident did you? You can see that yellow sign literally from miles away. You are not even looking in that direction and bingo!-there it is. Your eyes automatically go right to it.

How would you use this in your office? I would have all my trainers have the word TRAINER written in yellow right across their back. Do it with a red or light blue shirt. The members in the club will be getting "subliminal messaging" the entire time they are in the club. They will not be able to avoid the subliminal message of TRAINER. Before long, they will have the strangest urge to talk to a trainer, guaranteed!

There are many other colors that affect people's emotions, but these are the ones that really make a huge impact on your ability to COMMUNICATE with your client's and members.

Chapter Eleven
Thoughts, Feelings, Actions

• •

Well, I have one more section to cover before we get to the McGill-Built 12 step Method. This information is vitally important. This information has to do with YOU. What do you think of you? You see, if you are looking for the next great thing to make you a million dollars; the next great thing to really make your life COMPLETE; I have a secret to tell you. You already have what it takes to be successful. You also already have what it takes to fail. The ONLY thing that will ever really get you where you want to be is:

YOU, YOU, YOU, YOU, YOU, AND OH YA, YOU!

The techniques I have already shared with you, and all the other ones I am going to share with you, will only work if YOU BELIEVE IN YOU. Your success begins and ends with you! I just want to bring to your awareness some information that I really feel you need to know in order to make my techniques, or any techniques work for a lifetime of success. Let's discuss a few things - let's go!!

THOUGHTS, FEELINGS, ACTIONS

Phase I

1. Why are people, who are far less talented than you, accomplishing far more than you? The people that accomplish their dreams in this world are the people that "expect" what they want. They don't wish or hope for what they want. "You will always get what you expect, not what you want."

2. How do you view money? What is your first thought when you think of a million dollars? Most people's "real" view of money is far different than they tell their friends or family. People will usually say that when they think about money they get excited, but the reality is, that most people's thoughts about money are those of frustration and the lack of money. Until those change, you will always have reason to have frustration, and a lack of funds.

3. How do you view yourself as a parent, son/daughter, spouse, income earner, business person etc.? *The "me" I "see", is the "me" I will "be."* You must always have a good picture of yourself. You will never succeed beyond the "image" that you "see" in the mirror.

4. What does the phrase, "If I want more, I must become more" mean? You must always be growing so you can have the ability to perform at the next level. People always want more, but they seldom focus on their own growth. "YOU" must become "more" if "YOU" want "more".

5. Think about everyone in your life. Out of all the people in your life: kids, spouse, boss, in-laws, neighbors, etc., who REALLY needs to change for your life to get better? This is simple-YOU, YOU, YOU.

6. What does the phrase, "energy flows were attention goes" mean? You can only attract to you that energy which you are resonating with. You cannot split energy. That, which you focus on with feeling, is what you will manifest in your life- good or bad.

7. When you permit what is happening around you to determine how you think, then you become a play-thing for outside forces. Explain? Do not wait for all the lights in town to turn green before you get in your car. The external environment has nothing to do with your success. "When the vision on the inside is stronger than the circumstances on the outside, you have mastered your life."

Phase II

8. Why are you excellent at some things in your life, but lousy at other things? You are programmed to "believe" and "expect" the outcome of any situation. All you have to do, to get better at something, is change your expectation.

9. Do you think your thoughts have anything to do with where you are at this point of your life? Your thoughts have brought you where you are at this point in your life. The great thing about thought is, that it can go any way it wants in a fraction of a second. "What you did yesterday, you paid for- what you do today- you decide."

10. How do you spend your free time? The more you put in, the more you get out! Life is really simple in this manner.

11. What is the difference between motivation and inspiration? Motivation is external; inspiration is internal. You use someone else's energy to be motivated; you use your own energy to be inspired. Hint- if you need someone else's energy to do whatever it is that you are doing, then you need to quit doing it!!

12. Why do you do the things you do- good or bad- and why do you still keep doing them? We are all wired to do certain things. We need to change our "wired" connections. In technical terms- our Psycho-Cybernetic Mechanism. We are "programmed" by our repetitive exposure and actions to things, which in turn, forms our "habits." And we are also "programmed" do to our "dramatic" and "traumatic" experiences. "The neurons that "fire" together, "wire" together."

13. What do you REALLY want, (do not settle for less)? We often settle for less, because we have bought into everyone else's opinion of what our capabilities are. The hell with them. You can do, or be any one you choose-GO FOR IT! Whatever you did in the past,

"was what you did," it's "not who you are"- big difference! Don't let your past actions or results define "who you are".

14. What do you think is holding you back from getting what you REALLY want? Your belief in yourself! Our God given birthright is to have prosperity. NEVER for hard times. That's God's will for you, for me, and for the entire world. We've been conned folks - go get what you really want in this world. It is yours for the taking - Enjoy your life!

15. Do you REALLY believe you can have anything you want in life, or is that only for the "lucky and/or special people?" This needs to change for many of us. WE DESERVE OUR DREAMS.

16. What does the saying, "You are the average of the five people you spend the most time with," mean? Your surroundings will ultimately have an in-depth effect on you. You must do an inventory of those closest to you. See where they are headed. Are they going in the same direction as you? If not, than you have some decisions to make. I absolutely love many of my friends, but I do not spend the majority of my time with some of them. They simply are not going where I am going; not necessarily better or worse, just a different path.

Phase III

17. How do you handle failure? Ask a loser what failure has done to him, and he will tell you that it has ruined his life. "If it weren't for this person, or that situation, BLAH, BLAH, BLAH." Ask a successful person what failure has done for her, and she will tell you that it was the biggest asset in her life. Successful people find value and growth in everything in life. "Since we can expect to fail often in our lives; we are guaranteed a lot of growing opportunities."

18. What does the phrase, "protect you from yourself" mean?

Sometimes, we need to just get out of our own way. Hone your skills and manage your weaknesses. Be honest on the issues you need help with. The ONLY way to do this, when things are going in the wrong direction, is to LOOK IN THE MIRROR!

19. Why don't you do the things you know you should do, but you simply never get done? "Lack of confidence leads to procrastination, which leads to failure."

20. Why hasn't it worked out for you to have and keep money, even though you frequently think about "needing" and "wanting" money? Most people are programmed to "spend," not "save." Change the "picture" of what the "definition" of money should be. Make a game out of saving money. Quit playing the spending game!

21. What is the first thing you do with money when you get it? I think we just answered this in the last question.

22. Do you generally view other people as successful, but not yourself? "Envy is ignorance and imitation is suicide." Define your success by "your" value system, not someone else's definition of "their" value system.

23. Do you dislike, or fear "change?" "The only consistent thing is change." If you say to someone, "I like things just the way they are," that is a sign of ignorance. NOTHING ever stays the same. This would totally go against every natural law of the universe. You are either going forward or you are going backwards. All you have to do is ask yourself, "Am I going to step forward into growth, or step back into safety?" The problem is that the so called safe place has a paper floor - Watch where you are standing!

24. Do you make decisions on your own, or with the influence of others? When you are totally congruent with your vision, and you are in total harmony with the good you desire, you will only need

your "inner voice" of understanding.

25. Who has been the #1 reason for your success or failure in important areas of your life? Has it been more than one person? I believe we have covered this topic-YOU, YOU, YOU, YOU, AND OH YA, YOU.

I was giving a seminar in Florida recently to a group of very successful business people and I asked everyone in the room, "Who is the most instrumental person in your life that has had the biggest affect on your success?" I received a variety of different answers; everything from mom, dad, teachers, etc. One gentleman, a highly decorated veteran of the armed forces, and a very successful businessman, told me that his pastor was the biggest reason for his success. This gentleman grew up in the rough area of East St. Louis Missouri, not the most user friendly place to cultivate young people. I told him, I thought that was very nice that he would give that gentleman the credit for his success. Then I said, "That pastor really was not the reason for your success at all. In fact, all the answers that were given from all of you are incorrect!" You could have heard a pin drop! I referred to the gentleman that spoke of his pastor, and I said to him, "How many other children had the opportunity to experience this great man and pastor, that you had the opportunity to experience?" The gentleman said, "Well, hundreds that I personally know of. Our mothers and grandmothers would take us to church every Sunday. We also had weekly events at the church. There were a lot of kids in my neighborhood; I lived in a large area."Then I asked - How many of the other kids went on to do good or possibly great things? He had said, "Well, not too many at all. A lot of them got caught up into drugs; many are in prison, and some are already dead."

I said to this man, "Obviously, you are selling yourself short. You are the decision maker in your life, just as the other children were. You decided to allow this person to have a positive influence in your life; the other children had that opportunity as well. You and the other children also had the opportunity to allow the drug dealers and convicts to influence your lives, and from the sounds of it, many of the other children "chose" to head in that direction - Same opportunity to allow good to enter into a bunch of kids lives - drastically different results! Sir, you are to be commended for your strength and perseverance in a world that was far too easy to head in another direction."

I think the crowd got the point! Many of them sat up in their chairs with a new found sense of pride and respect for themselves. Not to make light of this statement at all; the fact is, we may not, at least at a young age, have full control over who is in our lives, but as we grow older, we darn sure have full control over whether we are going to involve ourselves in actions that are good or bad for us. The universe does not recognize other people, or "their energy" in "your life." The universe recognizes "your energy." It will bring other energy to you of "like a kind." Whatever energy you are resonating with, you will attract. The universe will not try to figure out if you have been wronged by someone, or if you feel you are a victim, it only recognizes the vibration you are in, and it will give it back to you 100 fold. It would be in your best interest to think and accept the situation as your ownership. Dr. Michael Beckwith said it best, "A thought is a unit of mental energy that can be measured scientifically. These thoughts transmute themselves through speech, behavior, and the effect of your life. Those thoughts ultimately become the feeling tone of your life. A person could actually generate a certain feeling of gratitude, love, peace, harmony, and OWNERSHIP. The universe will begin to match that feeling tone, and what will "flow" into your life will match the "feeling" you are holding. It is scientific, it's real. It means that everyone can release themselves from being a victim and begin to take control of their life's destiny. Your life is going to have a destiny anyway; you might as well control it instead of someone else." End of quote!

I am 45 years old now, and I can honestly say that I believe we all have the same opportunity to make choices; these choices will be very good for our future, or devastatingly bad for our future - We make the decisions! Be proud of your strength and conviction to be the best you can be. When you take control, you automatically have control. Of this you can be sure!

Chapter Twelve
The McGillBuilt 12 Step Method

Well, here we go. I am going to explain to you step by step the McGillBuilt Method.

CAUTION:
There are three versions that I teach, when explaining the Legendary McGillBuilt 12 Step Method. This version of the McGillBuilt 12 Step Method is the 1st phase, of three phases. This phase will give you a great idea on how to present the method, and will absolutely increase your income beyond what you may have thought possible. Having said this- the McGillBuilt 12 Step Method is so detailed, and complex, that because of all the other information in this book, I felt it would be overwhelming to have the 2nd or 3rd phases explained here. This phase is 16 pages, the 2nd phase is 50 pages, and the 3rd phase is 100 pages. Phase two is currently offered as a certification curriculum in 87 Countries around the World. The McGillBuilt 12 Step Method is legally labeled an "intellectual property," and is legally filed as such.
Please enjoy your learning experience. When you have completed studying the 12 Step Method, you will absolutely view the potential of your health and fitness career through a different set of glasses - Here we go!

We have discussed a lot of vital points so far. Because of that, when I am going through the 12 steps you should be able to reflect back on various sections, and visualize where certain techniques can be implemented. If this becomes an issue for you, you may want to go back through a few chapters to freshen up. Keep in mind, the "Open three doors to close one" format, and that will allow you to have an outline to go by. Most of the McGillBuilt 12 Step Method is focused on door number one - relax and relate. When relaxing and relating with your client is done properly, the "desire and disturb" door is very easy to open. People will not open up to you if they do not feel comfortable with you. You accomplish this comfort during the "relax and relate" stage; which as I said, is mainly throughout the entire presentation. There are two sections that we will focus on for the desire and disturb door. Section one: when we are reviewing their body part goals. Section two: when we are having them open up to us in the feelings section at the end of the evaluation.

Do not do the "feelings" portion at the beginning or in the middle. Doing the "feeling" portion at any time, other than at the end, is presentation suicide. TRUST, TRUST, TRUST ME ON THIS ONE!
I feel I must give this analogy concerning my point on the feeling step. Picture this: you and your spouse or lover are out on the town enjoying each others company; laughing dancing, and just having a good old time. Picture being on the dance floor with some soft music playing, Barry White, Luther Van dross, or something of that nature. The lights are dimly lit, and the mood was oh, so right! You start to whisper sweet nothings in your partners' ear. Things are starting to heat up; you cannot wait to get home and end the night with romantic bliss.

Now picture this; this moment on the dance floor is at its peak of, let's say, PASSION, EMOTION, AND DESIRE, somewhere around the fifth to the last song of the night.

Now, envision the D.J. turning the lights up, and starting to play, let's say - some other than romantic music- A.C.D.C.'s Highway to Hell, Nazareth's The Bitch is Back; maybe a little bit of Snoop Dog- you get the picture! WOW!! What a buzz kill. How romantic do you feel now? Can you recapture that feeling? Yes, perhaps, but the first time is the best time, if you know what I mean!

Now relating this to your evaluation presentation: Why wouldn't you wait and open this door when you can actually walk through it? This is exactly what I see people do when presenting their personal training service to a prospective client. They try to do the "feeling" section somewhere in the beginning or middle of the presentation, and then end up with the nuts and bolts, or dog and pony show at the end. The crazy thing is, when I have witnessed "sales people" trying to do the "feeling" portion of their "other" presentation, the sales person does a pathetic job, at best, even when they attempt the "feelings" section anywhere in the presentation. I call it "tickling the client under the arms." They just skim over the feeling section, just to say they did it. They need to get that portion "out of the way," so they can get to the "hard close" section – pardon my French – but what a bunch of dumb asses!

THIS IS THE SECTION THAT WILL MAKE OR BREAK YOU'RE POCKET BOOK, PERIOD!

Again, as we are going through these steps, picture yourself talking to your client about their kids - get names, and ages of anyone that has influence, or is special to them: spouse or partner, hobbies, interests, health concerns, etc. Any information about your client is valuable to you, if you want to be successful in opening door one and door two. I have seen so many sales people just go through the motions during their presentation, and then they wonder why they cannot close a deal. Remember, effective COMMUNICATION is done by asking the right questions and gathering as much personal information as possible.

Enough prepping; let's do an evaluation.

STEP ONE: QUESTIONNAIRE (RELAX AND RELATE)

This is really simple. Have your client fill out your questionnaire. There are key questions within the questionnaire that are vitally important to take note of so you can begin to build your information bank. Just like putting money in the bank, you want it in there so you can, at some point, draw it back out to use it for something that benefits you. The information that you are depositing in your information account will be needed very soon.

Key questions to look at after your client fills out the questionnaire:

1. Have you ever been a member of a health club before? If so, why did you cancel?

   A. You need to see if they stopped coming for money reasons, this will tip you off on their financial situation. This will help you have a head's up on the personal training program that may best fit their financial needs.

   B. You need to see if they quit because they didn't get any help or guidance while at the club. Remember, you are there to show them the value in your training team. You offer guidance, structure, and accountability.

People often quit fitness facilities because of these reasons: they get frustrated over not knowing what they are doing, and also from the lack of good direction from people in the club.

2. "Have you ever had trouble motivating your self?"
3. "What factors will help you reach your fitness goals?"
4. "What factors will keep you from reaching your fitness goals?"

These questions all coincide with what we just discussed in question one. Everything your training team offers can solve all these questions – this is valuable information to put in your account.

5. Another key question is; "Will your spouse or significant other

be working out with you, or supporting your goals?

Think about this one. The partner is very important in this process. We want the partner to be on board; this makes life a lot easier for everyone.

STEP TWO: BODY FAT %
(RELAX AND RELATE)

Simply do a body fat analysis. You want your client to get a good idea of the shape, or lack of shape they are in. The reality of your client's physical condition need's to be brought front and center during this step.

Key point: no matter how terrible the outcomes of the body fat percentage; always make sure your client realizes that you are able to help them make incredible improvements - Of course you know that you can - If you don't think so, then you shouldn't be working in the fitness industry. Your client needs to know that YOU BELIEVE in them, and also BELIEVE in your ability to get them there!

STEP THREE: WISH LIST
(BODY PART PICTURE)
(RELAX AND RELATE)
(BUILD SOME DESIRE)

This is when you help your client build a picture of what they want to physically look like. Ask your client this question, "Sally, if you could wake up tomorrow and have your body look any way that you wanted – describe how it would look?" Once they start to describe their perfect body, write it all down as clearly as possible. Really get detailed with this step. Don't just let them say, "I would like lose weight in my arms, legs, and stomach." No, that is not nearly enough of a picture for them to get excited about. They need to see the arms in this way, "Sally, do you want the back of your arms to be toned and firm? This part of your arm is called the triceps; would you like your bicep portion (actually touch your own bicep so she can visually see) of your arm to also be toned and firm?"

You are Picasso. You must paint as vivid of a picture as you possibly can. When you are done going through her entire body; Sally should have an actual snapshot in her mind of her perfect body.

This is the step that starts the feeling process ever so slowly. Still, we want to wake up Sally's ability to dream. We do not want her to get too emotionally excited yet - We still have the dog and pony show to go through.

STEP FOUR: DOG AND PONY SHOW (RELAX AND RELATE)

This step is the section where you can express your intelligence on basic fitness information. Explain about the human body relative to fitness. You can really do a lot of relating in this section. We are all subjected to the same basic human body realities. Eat too much sugar, and you will bounce off the walls. Sit around all day, and most of us will gain some unwanted weight. Eat greasy food all the time, and we will all have some heart issues sooner or later. This goes for the good things as well. Exercise regularly and we will feel better. Strength train with weights, and we will gain lean muscle tissue. Run on a treadmill for 20 minutes, and we will burn a fair amount of calories, etc., etc.

We are all in this fitness thing together. "Nobody gets out alive." I know that sounds terrible, but we can all really relate to our mortal existence. As you are explaining what you can help them with during their fitness journey; be sure to be relatable in the fact that we are going through our own physical journey, just as they are. This is a good bonding time. You can show your stuff when it comes to understanding how you can benefit them.

CAUTION:

Do not talk forever during the dog and pony show. This section is important, but it should never dominate the presentation. This step should be 15 minutes maximum. If your dog and pony show is formatted nicely, you can cover a lot of ground in 15 minutes or less. REMEMBER: "information makes you think, emotion make you act!" When you were in high school, did you feel more "fired up" after a rock concert, or after study hall?

GET THE PICTURE!!

STEP FIVE: PLATEAU AND CHANGE
(RELAX AND RELATE)

This step is bringing to your client's awareness, the fact that the human body needs "change." The human body will get used to anything, when it is physically repeating it over and over again, for an extended period of time. When it comes to exercise, this period of time is generally 4 to 6 weeks.

This section is to let your client know, that no matter what great routine you have, your body will absolutely get used to it in a relatively short period of time. This is why your client needs YOU, and your training team. Everyone can get a routine out of a fitness book - big deal. Hardly anyone knows how to put routines together, so they will interact with the previous routine. This is where your training teams' value comes in.

Once I show them the fact that their body will plateau, and changing their routine on a consistent bases is vital for their continued success; then I would say, "Sally, now that you know you need to change your routines, this still doesn't mean you know how to change your routine, does it?" I always received the answer that I was looking for, "No Duane, I have no idea how to do that." That's OK Sally, that's what I am here for."

STEP SIX: WHAT YOU WILL DO FOR THEM (RELATE AND RELAX)
(A LITTLE BIT OF DOOR THREE "SOLUTION")

Once you have reviewed the fact that your client does not know how to put together consistent routines for herself, and that just happens to be YOUR strong point, then you can explain to her what you will do for her.

STRUCTURED WORKOUTS:
"Sally, we are going to structure all of your workouts (pull out workout card), we are going to structure your sets, reps, and machines so you do not have to worry about any of that. Before or after a hard day of work, the last thing you want to do is have to organize a workout program, so we will take care of that for you. Sally, we are going to keep track of your routines on these workout cards."

MONTHLY EVALUATIONS:
We are going to give you monthly evaluations. Remember, what I said Sally; your body is going to plateau in about four to six weeks. This is why we want to catch it at about the four week mark, to make sure that we can keep your body moving in a forward direction. We will change your routine at this time."

NUTRITIONAL COACHING:
"Sally, we also offer nutritional coaching. Your eating habits are

going to play an incredible role in your physical success. How are your eating habits?"

At this point, let them talk your ear off. You have been speaking quite a lot; let them talk. They will tell you all sorts of things about their eating habits. Regardless of what they say; end with, "Well Sally, we are going to get you headed in the right direction in this area. Don't get me wrong Sally, we are not going to come into your house with our refrigerator and throw yours out. You wouldn't let us do that any way; we are going to be able to meet in the middle somewhere on your eating habits."

TEAM OF TRAINERS:

"Sally, we also have a team of trainers. I am the head trainer, and we also have a phenomenal team of trainers that can help you get all the results you are looking for, and you will have the option of having our personal training guidance before you leave here today if you choose too.

ROAD MAP FOR SUCCESS:

"Sally, WHEN you join our training team, we will lay a road map out for your success, step by step, to guarantee your results."

STEP SEVEN: WORKOUT EVALUATION (RELAX AND RELATE)

"Before we go any farther Sally, I need to see what I am working with. I don't know if I should put you on a beginner, middle of the road, or advanced routine. So I would like to go out on the workout floor and evaluate four things: strength, balance, coordination, and endurance. When we are done with this, we will come back in here, go over the results, and go from there. Sound good Sally?"

At this point, I simply take Sally through a workout, and evaluate her performance. I do this with a clip board and a blank sheet of white paper, and I write everything down with a black pen. I have them walk briskly on the treadmill for about six minutes. This will tell me if they have really bad endurance.

I basically do five exercises: Ball squats (for thighs, butt, and hamstrings); this is a good strength movement.
Weighted lunges (for thighs, hamstrings, and balance); these are excellent for evaluation balance. Dumbbell shoulder presses (for shoulders, and coordination); these are great for coordination. Lateral raises (for side deltoids) good strength movement. Vertical crunches, for upper and lower mid section.

The evaluation is over at this point. I bring Sally back in the office. I review her results. I am very real with her results. I actually grade the exercises A thru D. If Sally did very well with all the exercises, I would say, "You did excellent on your evaluation Sally." What this tells me is that I am going to be able to put you on a more advanced routine to ALLOW YOU TO GET RESULTS FASTER."
People love the thought of getting fast results. Now, she is really fired up!

If Sally didn't do very well, then this is also O. K. "Sally, I know I am not telling you something you don't already know, but we have some things to work on. But that's O.K; you already knew you needed some help. That's why you're here, and we are going to provide you with the help you need to reach your fitness goals."

Either way, Sally QUALIFIES for the training team.
Your client should ALWAYS feel like they have hope. I have seen every conceivable "physical challenge," and they are ALL within reach of concurring. "I see only the objective, the obstacles must give way."
As a health and fitness professional, this should ABSOLUTELY be

you're "thought" process!

STEP EIGHT: FEELINGS, BLUE PAPER (DESIRE AND DISTURB)

This is THE STEP OF ALL STEPS. This is what you have been building up to through the entire evaluation. If you opened the "relax and relate" door correctly throughout your evaluation, then the "desire and disturb" door will open nicely. Remember when I said, "You have to capture the "feeling portion" at the end of your evaluation?" Well, there are four more steps after this step, but they are basically sub-steps of the "feeling" step; you will see what I mean in a moment.

O. K., after you have reviewed the workout evaluation; make sure you have everything off your desk, other than the stack of papers that you have been using up to this point. You will be referring back to some of them in a moment. Take your light blue paper, and put it over the top of the stack of other papers. Nothing else should be on the desk AT ALL. You want Sally's full attention on the blue paper.

This is how you will start, "Sally, what I would like to do now, is talk about the REAL reason you are here. I would like to discuss your goals and your values as they pertain to getting physically fit. Sally everyone wants to get in shape, everyone wants to tone up and lose weight; you didn't invent that; but Sally, people want to get in shape for a lot of different reason's. Nobody wants to tone up or lose weight just for the sake of the scales reading a different set of numbers, or their body being a little more defined. There is something behind the superficial reason. Some people exercise because of health issues, if not their own, there may be some in the family, and they don't want to inherit the family curse. Other people do it for self confidence, self esteem, their career, or their family - What are they for you?"

TIMEOUT; can you see now why you needed to relax and relate

to your client, become their friend and COMMUNICATE with them on a level of THEIR understanding? Do you see how blunt I am on my approach to getting them to share with me their deep rooted feelings? This is not JUST going to happen if people do not FEEL comfortable with you. YOU HAVE TO EARN THE RIGHT TO ASK FOR THIS INFORMATION. If you didn't do your job on EARNING the right to go this deep, then you don't deserve to have your client join your team.

O. K., back to business; you have gathered a lot of information that you have waiting for you in your information account. Remember, it is time to withdrawal this information a little at a time. Sally starts saying a few things; fairly superficial things in the beginning. She will not know just how deep you want to go. As she realizes that you want to know the real emotional reasons, then she will proceed to talk more.

As Sally is listing her reasons, you will be writing them down on your light blue paper with your red sharpie marker. You will write the sentence as Sally says it. Example: "I want to be alive to see Josh graduate." You will write that sentence just as it came out of Sally's mouth. It is vital that you do it this way. The paper is going to be facing Sally; she will be reading it time and time again as she is sitting there thinking of her other desires. This becomes Sally's crystal ball. I talked about this earlier; Sally will become mesmerized by her own words.

When Sally is at the apex of her EMOTION, PASSION, AND DESIRES, it will be obvious to you. Often people start to cry, heck many times I started to tear up. This is a very serious time for people. This is a crossroads for their life. For many people the reasons are serious. I am not just talking about having a beach body for summer. When people really "open up" to you, it is amazing what is lying deep inside them. I know it doesn't take long for me to get emotional when I am talking about what is truly important in my life. We are all the same in this respect. Sure, there may be some sociopaths out there that don't feel, but they are few and far between. The rest of us are a bunch of softies. Heck, I have had 30 year old, 20 inch armed, barrel chest studs, crying at my table. This technique is fair game for any of us.

Anyway, when Sally is fully in the zone on the desires of her heart, you will want to disturb the situation. You were probably wondering when we were going to get to this part. Well, here we are, this is what you do next; ask this question, "Sally, what would happen if you couldn't have all these things that you want?" Verbally list all the items on the paper, stare right at them. You will notice a fear in Sally's eyes; she will say, "I must have them!"

"People get a feeling, and then they purchase the feeling." Do not ever forget this.

STEP NINE: 2 FOR 2
(DESIRE)

At this point you will say, "Sally, so you are serious about reaching your goals?" YES! "O. K. Sally do you see value in personal training guidance to help you reach your goals?" (List the goals from the blue paper one by one). Yes, Sally says, "Well Sally you are two for two – you see, if you were serious about your goals, but you didn't see value in personal training guidance to help you reach your goal, I couldn't give it to you for free, could I?" NO! "And Sally, if you saw value in personal training guidance, but you were not serious about reaching your goals, I couldn't give you personal training for free this way either, could I?" NO! "So, since you are two for two, I would like to show you some session options that we have available to you. Would you like to see some session options Sally?" YES!!

STEP TEN: SESSION OPTIONS (DESIRE)

Verbally explain the options at a normal speed. There is no reason to "visually" show the prices. Very few people need to "see" the price options. If you are sitting in front of an extreme "visual" personality type, you will have to show some numbers, but this is a small percentage of the time. Leave ONLY the blue paper in front of Sally. When Sally is making her decision on which package to choose, you want her focus to be on why she is there, not on the expense. Think about it this way; when you are at a store, and you are deciding whether to make a fairly large purchase; as you are staring at the price sheet, what else is going through your mind? Think real hard? Your phone bill, your car payment, your grocery bill, your car and house insurance, and or your apartment rent, right? The last thing you want Sally to be reviewing is her debt load. If we always focus on this, we would never buy anything.

Don't get me wrong, I do not want to Sally join the training team on a program that she cannot afford, but I do want her to do whatever she can do to rearrange some finances in order to change her life. I guarantee you this; Sally probably wastes a fair amount of money each month like the rest of us do. I was in the finance business for many, many years, and I am here to tell you; we waste a fair share of our income.

I said this before; the average American has only saved $10,000 after 40 years of working. This tells me one very important thing; if Sally doesn't spend her money on changing her life for the better, she is going to leave here, go over to the mall, and find something to spend her money on. If you think there is something better for Sally's health at the mall, then you better go work at the mall!!

STEP ELEVEN: AGREEMENT (DESIRE)

This step is the easiest door to close in the world. Just fill out the agreement, NOT CONTRACT. Position the agreement in such a way, that you can fill out the information without your client staring at it. You only have the blue paper in front of Sally. At least for a minute, then you put her to work on a little project while you are tidying up the formalities.

STEP TWELVE: THREE DAY FOOD LIST

This is a list of everything they have eaten in the last three days. This is done for two reasons. First, you need to give this to Sally's trainer so he or she can immediately start working on Sally's nutritional package. Second, it is a great way to get Sally quickly involved in the process of getting fit, and not having her stare at the agreement, and start having second thoughts. Sometimes, you just have to protect people from themselves. You just continue to wrap up the paperwork, and Sally will be totally engrossed in her food journal- all is good!! The only thing you do now is get Sally's payment preference; cash, check, or charge.

Please remember – you must make sure your client purchases an affordable personal training package. There is no value in having them join your training team for a month, and then have to quit because they can't afford the option they chose.

A JOB WELL DONE-ON TO THE NEXT PERSON THAT GETS' THE OPPORTUNITY TO JOIN YOUR TRAINING TEAM!

Chapter Thirteen
G.M. REPORT CARD

This chapter is really a bonus chapter. I would like to give you a format on how to gauge your success as a manager of a fitness club. I have developed a report card for areas that you may want to pay close attention to. This will help you stay on the right track when reviewing all that your job entails.

G.M. Report Card

1. Office organization (clean, paperwork, professional appearance) - Grade
2. Computer skills – Grade
3. Punctuality to club – Grade
4. Customer service (attitude) - Grade
5. Customer service (Skill level) – Grade
6. Ownership to G.M. position – Grade
7. Phone ability (voice, excitement, message content) – Grade
8. Appointment setting (desire and willingness) – Grade
9. Appointment setting (success) – Grade
10. Appointment setting (show %) – Grade
11. Understanding company system – Grade
12. Presenting company system – Grade
13. Appointment book up to date (joined, no deal, be backs, reschedule, no show, etc.) – Grade
14. Follow up on straggler deals (sign c.c. receipt, money down later, contract mishaps) – Grade
15. Working the floor (mingling, being a present in club) – Grade

16. Organizing trainers (Right clients with right trainer, checking schedules, appearance, etc) – Grade

17. Applying learned information (what I, and the company are teaching them) – Grade

18. Remembering deals (sold deals, be back deals, anything to do with the MONEY) - Grade

19. Deal average – Grade

20. Gross (ability to get P.I.F) "Paid in full" – Grade

21. Down payment – Grade

22. Work out prospective clients as to show value – Grade

23. Overcoming objections – Grade

24. Flow of filling out agreement at the table – Grade

25. Belief in company value – Grade

26. Belief in ability to sell company program– Grade

27. Psychology of sales (round table, colors, mirroring, proximities, hypnotic language patterns, etc.) – Grade

28. Universal laws (mind set, self talk, resonating energy, internalizing, etc.) – Grade

Rating System

   A. 4 points   Possible points – 112
   B. 3 points   A. 112 – 89.6
   C. 3 points   B. 89.5 – 67.2
   D. 2 points   C. 67.1 – 44.8
   E. 1 point   D. 44.7 – 22.4
   F. 0 points   E. 22.3 – 0

The lower "A" level should always produce 75 to 90% of goal.

A G.M. at the middle to lower "B" level should normally do 50 to 60 % of goal.

Well, I am sure you are going to do excellent with this information and I trust that you will respect the power which you have been shown. I will be available for seminars throughout the country. I look forward to working with you in the very near future.

Have a great and prosperous life; as I know you will.

Duane McGill
President and Founder
McGillBuilt Fitness Systems, Inc.

Contact Information
Duane McGill
Web: http://www.McGillBuilt.com
Email: Duane@McGillBuilt.com
Toll Free: (877)533-8156

Testimonial...

Ever since I was an adolescent I was prone to trouble and negativity. When I first met Duane I was a personal trainer at Golds Gym just trying to make a living. I had moved out of my previous hometown because I had gotten into trouble, and I figured that moving to a new town would give me a new start. However, I felt as though, sooner or later, I would go back to my old ways, but then I met Duane, and he inspired me to look at life in a different perspective. Now I look at life in a different way, it doesn't matter about my past, it only matters about the future. So now everyday I wake up and I tell myself that I am a genius and I plan my wisdom everyday. I read positive books, I surround myself with positive people, I go to church, and I attract positive energy from the universe. Just because you came from a bad back ground or past, doesn't mean you cant change and have a phenomenal life. Thank You Duane.

- Jason Wildes, Grateful Student

Testimonial...

The first time I met Duane McGill was back in October of 2008. I was working as the Fitness Director at Fitness 1 gym in Surprise Arizona. I had never met Duane in person but I had been on a conference call with him set up by Custom Built a few months earlier. I was told by my employer that they were bringing Duane on board to help restructure our way of thinking on how to sell and service the members at our gym.

I had heard great things about Duane and what he had done for other companies. To be honest I didn't really believe all the hype that went along with him. He was talked about like the All Mighty himself. I almost felt like he was royalty of some sort and that I should bow to him when he walked through the doors to our gym. I had been in the fitness industry for almost 18 years, was very established, and also had done many great things in the past as far as selling training. I had set records at almost every gym I had ever sold training in and truly felt the way I sold training and serviced members was the best way. I had my doubts anyone else would be able to show me a better way. I only tell this story not to brag about me, but to brag about the difference Duane McGill made in my life not only as a salesperson/trainer.

When I first laid eyes on Duane McGill my initial thought was that he had the look of an old drill sergeant from the military. I thought oh boy here we go. This guy is going to strong arm me into some old school bullshit on how to relate to people and get them to buy training, like I didn't already know how to do that. Boy was I wrong.

Not only did Duane teach me how to NOT be a salesperson, but how to actually care about the people I sat in front of. He told me it was an honor and privilege for these people to let us in to their world and to never take for granted the opportunity they are giving us to help them. It didn't matter if they purchased training with us or not. It was about taking the time to listen to them and truly care about why they joined the gym. For many people it is more than skin deep. Duane taught me it is a very emotional reason why most people join a club and to be very gentle and never dismiss anyone's feelings. The consultation is not about us but about them. God gave us two ears and one mouth for a reason. Talk less and listen more.

Duane's big thing was teaching people to become a Master Communicator NOT a salesperson. People hate salespeople. They want someone who actually cares about their needs and wants. Not someone that just nods there head and agrees with every word they say just to get them to purchase a product.

I could sit and talk about all the awesome things Duane taught me about work and making more money but that's not what I really took away from the short 2 months I worked with Duane. What I remember most about Duane is how he taught me to be a better man, a better person, a better friend, a better husband, a better dad. He taught me how to look at work as a place to come and have fun. He taught me how to try and enjoy work and not dread going to my job every day. He also taught me to not take work home. He always said to go home and enjoy my family, don't stress about what happened or didn't happen at work today. It will still be there for you to deal with tomorrow.

Duane preached to me a lot about the Laws of attraction. You attract positive and negative situations based on your thought patterns. He is so right. I had never had someone tell me that before. Not only did he tell me that but he was able to show me and prove it to me.

A lot of people in the industry talk a lot of shit about ways to do things and how this way or that way will help you sell more or make more money, but Duane is the only person I have seen that can prove his way of doing things is not only better but ETHICAL. They help you live a better life, not only on the outside but on the inside too. He taught me how to feel good about putting people "ON THE TEAM" that's what Duane called it when we signed someone up for personal training. People like to be on a team, to know they are part of something. Most people are scared and intimidated by the gym and don't want to be singled out. So Duane teaches you the right way to COMMUNICATE with humans, and how to speak in their language, how to put yourself in their shoes and try to understand how they feel.

Not only did he want us to do that at work, but he taught me how to do that with people in general.

I will say Duane and I hit it off from day one. I still remember sitting in our little office in the Fitness 1 gym and we talked not about work but about our lives growing up. Wouldn't you know it; we were brought up a lot the same. Our families were a lot alike. Our values and morals were the same. It was almost like we could be brothers and that was scary!

I have been around the world and worked in many different gyms and even had a few different careers. Never in my life have I come in contact with someone that has changed my life the way Duane McGill changed mine!

I do believe one of the last things I told Duane is my experience with him was probably something like the 12 Disciples had with Jesus Christ. Duane can help you move mountains. He doesn't allow negative thinking and he doesn't allow you to get down on yourself.

One of the most amazing things about Duane is he is a family man. He always believed in family comes first. I think every day I was around Duane he talked about his family and how much they mean to him and his success. That is very rare in today's society. Most owners of companies don't give 2 shits about you or your family. It's all about the company and how much money you can make them. Duane says bullshit to that thought process.

Employers need to learn and old theory. Take care of those that take care of you. Without the grunts and people considered as ground zero employees. Their doors would close and those rich business owners wouldn't be living the lifestyles of the Rich and Famous.

I could go on and on for days about the difference Duane has made in my life. I thank God every day that we crossed paths. My only wish as that there were more Duane McGill's to go around. The world would be a much better place. All I know is that I hope I make the same impact on people's lives that Duane has made in mine. If you ever get a chance to meet Duane it will be an experience you will never forget.

Thanks again Duane for all that you have done for me and my family. Love you to death Brutha.

Love and Peace,

Blaine Radke